Easy Home Preserving

Jean Paré

www.companyscoming.com
visit our ↑ website

Back Cover

Left:
Nectarine Jam, page 76

Right:
1. Smoky Pear Salsa, page 23
2. Eggplant Salsa, page 45

Copyright © 2013 by Company's Coming Publishing Limited

First printed in 2013   10 9 8 7 6 5 4 3

Printed in China

Library and Archives Canada Cataloguing in Publication
Paré, Jean, date
Easy home preserving / Jean Paré.
(Original series)
Includes index.
At head of title: Company's Coming.
ISBN 978-1-927126-52-3
 1. Canning and preserving. 2. Cookbooks. I. Title.
II. Series: Paré, Jean, date. Original series.
 TX603.P365 2013   641.4'2   C2012-907735-6

Front cover: The Weck Canada preserve and syrup jars on pages 54, 71, 125, 143, 144 and on the front cover were donated generously by Jade W.

Published by
Company's Coming Publishing Limited
87 East Pender Street
Vancouver, British Columbia, Canada V6A 1S9
Tel: 604-687-5555   Fax: 604-687-5575
www.companyscoming.com

Company's Coming is a registered trademark owned by Company's Coming Publishing Limited

We acknowledge the financial support of the Government of Canada through the Canada Book Fund for our publishing activities.

 Canadian   Patrimoine
Heritage   canadien

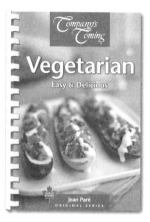

Table of Contents

The Company's Coming Story

Jean Paré (pronounced "jeen PAIR-ee") grew up understanding that the combination of family, friends and home cooking is the best recipe for a good life. From her mother, she learned to appreciate good cooking, while her father praised even her earliest attempts in the kitchen. When Jean left home, she took with her a love of cooking, many family recipes and an intriguing desire to read cookbooks as if they were novels!

"Never share a recipe you wouldn't use yourself."

When her four children had all reached school age, Jean volunteered to cater the 50th anniversary celebration of the Vermilion School of Agriculture, now Lakeland College, in Alberta, Canada. Working out of her home, Jean prepared a dinner for more than 1,000 people, launching a flourishing catering operation that continued for over 18 years. During that time, she had countless opportunities to test new ideas with immediate feedback—resulting in empty plates and contented customers! Whether preparing cocktail sandwiches for a house party or serving a hot meal for 1,500 people, Jean Paré earned a reputation for great food, courteous service and reasonable prices.

As requests for her recipes increased, Jean was often asked the question, "Why don't you write a cookbook?" Jean responded by teaming up with her son, Grant Lovig, in the fall of 1980 to form Company's Coming Publishing Limited. The publication of *150 Delicious Squares* on April 14, 1981 marked the debut of what would soon become one of the world's most popular cookbook series.

The company has grown since those early days when Jean worked from a spare bedroom in her home. Nowadays every Company's Coming recipe is *kitchen-tested* before it is approved for publication.

Company's Coming cookbooks are distributed in Canada, the United States, Australia and other world markets. Bestsellers many times over in English, Company's Coming cookbooks have also been published in French and Spanish.

Familiar and trusted in home kitchens around the world, Company's Coming cookbooks are offered in a variety of formats. Highly regarded as kitchen workbooks, the softcover Original Series, with its lay-flat plastic comb binding, is still a favourite among readers.

Jean Paré's approach to cooking has always called for *quick and easy recipes* using *everyday ingredients.* That view has served her well. The recipient of many awards, including the Queen Elizabeth Golden Jubilee Medal, Jean was appointed Member of the Order of Canada, her country's highest lifetime achievement honour.

Jean continues to share what she calls The Golden Rule of Cooking: *Never share a recipe you wouldn't use yourself.* It's an approach that has worked—*millions of times over!*

Foreword

In my grandmother's day, preserving food was a necessity to economize and to ensure an abundant winter food supply. Most families with a traditional rural background have a history of preserving their harvest of fruits and vegetables. Over the years, as more commercially canned products became available, preserving foods in the home became less important.

Today, we have come full circle. There is very strong renewed interest by many to preserve fresh garden produce, not only for enjoyment and fulfillment, but also for the confidence in knowing exactly what is in every jar—fresh food, prepared by you, without unnecessary additives or chemicals. My own family takes great enjoyment in the delicious foods that line my pantry shelves. No need to be intimidated—these recipes are easy and do not require an overwhelming time commitment. All recipes call for small quantities of ingredients.

If fresh fruits or vegetables are not in season when you want to make jam or jelly, you may substitute fresh frozen ones that do not have any water or sugar added. To get started, check the list on page 8 for basic equipment required.

A recognized source of reliable information on home food preservation in North America is the United States Department of Agriculture (USDA). In an effort to minimize food loss owing to spoilage in high acid foods such as jams, jellies and pickles, the USDA recommends the additional step of processing in a boiling water bath.

Preserving foods gives one a rewarding sense of accomplishment. So much enjoyment will surely come from making and serving these special extras to family and friends, or when presenting them as a gift from your kitchen—especially when you can say with pride: "I made it myself."

Jean Paré

Nutrition Information Guidelines

Each recipe is analyzed using the most current versions of the Canadian Nutrient File from Health Canada, and the United States Department of Agriculture (USDA) Nutrient Database for Standard Reference.

- If more than one ingredient is listed (such as "butter or hard margarine"), or if a range is given (1 – 2 tsp., 5 – 10 mL), only the first ingredient or first amount is analyzed.
- For meat, poultry and fish, the recommended serving size per person is 4 oz. (113 g) uncooked weight (without bone), which is 2 – 3 oz. (57 – 85 g) cooked weight (without bone)—approximately the size of a deck of playing cards.
- Milk used is 1% M.F. (milk fat), unless otherwise stated.
- Cooking oil used is canola oil, unless otherwise stated.
- Ingredients indicating "sprinkle," "optional" or "for garnish" are not included in the nutrition information.
- The fat in recipes and combination foods can vary greatly depending upon the sources and types of fats used in each specific ingredient. For these reasons, the amount of saturated, monounsaturated and polyunsaturated fats may not add up to the total fat content.

Equipment

Blender and/or Food Processor: Use either appliance to chop, slice or purée food.

Canner: A large deep kettle with a rack or false bottom that keeps jars off the bottom of the pan. A lid is included. Holds 7 jars. Use to process jars in a boiling water bath.

Cone-Shaped Food Mill: Use to separate pulp from purée. It will also hold a jelly bag for draining juices from fruit.

Dutch Oven: Use enamel-clad cast iron cookware for best results. Unlined cast iron may react with acidic foods to produce an off flavour or discolouration. The heavy bottom is necessary to disperse the heat evenly and prevent scorching when making jams and chutneys.

Food Grinder: Use to grind fruit rinds for marmalades or vegetables for relishes so they don't become too mushy.

Jar Tongs: To lift hot jars by their necks.

Jars: This book uses three jar sizes: 1/2 cup (125 mL) jars, 1 cup (250 mL) jars and 2 cup (500 mL) jars.

Labels: Use to identify the contents and to date each jar. Add a batch number (#1 or #2) if more than one batch is made in a single day. This can help eliminate bad batches if one jar spoils.

Large Saucepan or Preserving Pan: Aluminum or stainless steel saucepans are suitable to use and should be large enough to hold four times the volume to be cooked. Fully enamel saucepans are not recommended as they get very hot and cause food to scorch. The pan must be large enough to allow for the huge expansion when cooking jelly at a full rolling boil. It should also be wide enough to allow for rapid evaporation of liquid when boiling down jams, chutneys, etc.

Lids: The two-piece self-sealing metal lid consisting of a flat metal lid held in place by a metal screw band is the best choice. One side of the flat lid is crimped around its bottom edge to form a trough, which is filled with a coloured gasket compound, also known as a plastic sealing compound. When jars are processed, the lid gasket softens and flows slightly to cover the jar-sealing surface, yet allows air to escape from the jar. The gasket forms an airtight seal as the jar cools. Unused lids work well for about five years from the date of manufacture. Used lids should be discarded, as well as lids that are dented, deformed or flawed. Metal screw bands are good to reuse unless rusty.

Plastic Freezer Containers: Use sturdy plastic containers with tight-fitting lids, or short wide-mouthed freezer jars made specifically for jams and jellies, typically no larger than 2 cups (500 mL). Make sure containers have no leaks or cracks.

Scale: A small kitchen scale is a useful item. It should be able to weigh up to 5 or 6 pounds (2.5 to 3 kg) of food.

Spice Bag: A double layer cheesecloth bag can be used for whole spices. A solid cotton bag should be used if spice mixture contains seeds, so they won't go through the cloth.

Spoons: Long-handled spoons are best for deep-pot stirring and slotted spoons for removing food from hot liquid.

Tongs: To lift lids from hot water.

Unbleached Cotton and Cheesecloth: To make jelly bags and spice bags.

Vinegar: Always use good quality vinegar. White vinegar for pickling is at least 5% acetic acid by volume. All recipes were tested using 5% acetic acid vinegar unless stated otherwise. If vinegar is too weak or diluted, pickles will be soft and may not keep. White vinegar gives better colour when light coloured foods such as onions, ripe cucumbers, cauliflower or pears are used. Cider or malt vinegar is used when a special flavour is desired.

Wide Mouth Metal Canning Funnel: A big help for filling jars. It fits inside the neck of the jar and keeps the jar rims clean.

Glossary

Air Bubbles: After filling jars with food, release air bubbles by inserting a flat plastic (not metal) spatula between the food and the jar. Slowly turn the jar to move the spatula up and down to allow air bubbles to escape. Adjust the headspace and then clean the jar rim (sealing surface) with a dampened paper towel.

Boiling Water Bath: The United States Department of Agriculture (USDA) recommends the boiling water bath method for the final preserving step for high acid foods. Half fill canner with hot water. Place jars in rack. Lower rack to bottom. Pour in enough boiling water (not directly onto jars) to cover tops with 1 inch (2.5 cm) of water. Cover. Bring to a boil. Start timing for the number of minutes required to process the food. *Correct process time at higher elevations by adding one (1) additional minute per 1000 feet (305 m) above sea level.* Lower the heat to maintain a gentle boil. If needed, add boiling water to keep up the level. Foods such as fruits and tomatoes with high acid content should always be processed in a boiling water bath. See also: Sealing Jars.

Fruit: Since under-ripe fruit contains more pectin than ripe fruit, try to include some if possible when making jams, jellies and marmalades. This will aid in setting or jelling. Marmalade can take a week to set, jellies up to 24 hours.

Jelly Didn't Set: A quick remedy is to melt down the jelly until hot. Soften one 1/4 oz. (7 g) envelope unflavoured gelatin in 1/4 cup (50 mL) water for 1 minute. Stir into hot jelly to dissolve. This will set about 3 cups (750 mL) jelly. Re-bottle in re-sterilized jars. Jelly must now be kept in refrigerator for no longer than about one month. Another solution to this problem is to use the un-set jelly as pancake syrup.

Pectin: A naturally starchy substance found in fruit that causes jams and jellies to set. It is formed during ripening, but loses its gelling ability if the fruit becomes overripe. Commercial pectin is available in liquid or crystal form.

Rolling Boil: A boil that cannot be stirred down.

Sealing Jars: To seal a screw-top jar with metal lid, sterilize the lid in boiling water for 5 minutes and place the lid on the jar immediately after filling with the hot mixture being processed. Screw the metal band on securely, but do not tighten. Process in a boiling water bath. Do not retighten lids after processing jars. As jars cool, the contents in the jar contract, pulling the self-sealing lid firmly against the jar to form a vacuum seal. After the jars have cooled, you may remove the metal screw bands and store.

Processing jams, jellies and pickles in a boiling water bath is added assurance against spoilage. Fill sterilized mason jars with hot product, leaving 1/4 inch (0.5 cm) head space for 1 cup (250 mL) jars and 1/2 inch (1 cm) for 2 cup (500 mL) jars. Seal with self-sealing lids and process in a boiling water bath according to recipe.

In days gone by, jams and jellies were often sealed using paraffin wax. This is no longer recommended owing to possible mould contamination.

Sterilizing: Jars can be washed, rinsed and sterilized in the dishwasher. Set the dishwasher for the highest water temperature. The jars can also be sterilized in boiling water. Wash in hot soapy water and rinse well. Invert jars in 3 to 4 inches (7 to 10 cm) of boiling water in a large saucepan. Allow to boil for 10 minutes. Leave jars in water until you are ready to fill them. Fill jars while they are still hot. Wipe rims with clean paper towel, dipped in boiling water.

Citrusy Apricot Curd

This sweet, tangy and bright apricot curd can be used as a sauce and drizzled over cheesecakes, or simply spread over scones or French toast. This also makes a great filling for cakes or profiteroles.

Chopped peeled apricot (see Tip, page 129)	2 cups	500 mL
Lemon juice	1/4 cup	60 mL
Granulated sugar	1 cup	250 mL
Butter (or hard margarine), cut up	1/2 cup	125 mL
Orange juice	1/4 cup	60 mL
Grated lemon zest (see Tip, page 31)	1 tsp.	5 mL
Grated orange zest (see Tip, page 31)	1 tsp.	5 mL
Large eggs	6	6

Process apricot and lemon juice in food processor until smooth. Transfer to medium saucepan.

Add next 5 ingredients. Heat and stir on medium for about 5 minutes until sugar is dissolved and butter is melted. Remove from heat.

Beat eggs in medium heatproof bowl until frothy. Slowly add apricot mixture, stirring constantly. Return to saucepan. Heat and stir on medium for about 10 minutes until mixture is thick enough to coat back of a spoon. Do not boil. Strain through sieve into small bowl. Discard solids. Fill clean plastic containers to within 1/2 inch (12 mm) of top (see Tip, page 79). Wipe rims. Cover with plastic wrap directly on surface to prevent skin from forming. Chill until cool. Remove plastic wrap. Cover with tight-fitting lids. Store in refrigerator for up to 1 week or in freezer for up to 3 months. Makes about 3 3/4 cups (925 mL).

1 tbsp. (15 mL): 35 Calories; 2 g Total Fat (0.5 g Mono, 0 g Poly, 1 g Sat); 15 mg Cholesterol; 4 g Carbohydrate; 0 g Fibre; trace Protein; 15 mg Sodium

Strawberry Margarita Curd

This thick and creamy curd tastes as sweetly pink as it looks—and it requires just a few simple ingredients plus a little tequila. Use it as a cake filling or a topping for cheesecake, or spread it over muffins or biscuits.

Sliced fresh strawberries	2 cups	500 mL
Granulated sugar	1 cup	250 mL
Butter (or hard margarine), cut up	1/2 cup	125 mL
Lime juice	1/2 cup	125 mL
Tequila	2 tbsp.	30 mL
Large eggs	6	6

Process strawberries in blender or food processor until smooth. Transfer to medium saucepan.

Add next 4 ingredients. Heat and stir on medium for about 5 minutes until sugar is dissolved and butter is melted. Remove from heat.

Beat eggs in medium heatproof bowl until frothy. Slowly add strawberry mixture, stirring constantly. Return to saucepan. Heat and stir on medium for about 7 minutes until mixture is thick enough to coat back of a spoon. Do not boil. Strain through sieve into small bowl. Discard solids. Fill clean plastic containers to within 1/2 inch (12 mm) of top (see Tip, page 79). Wipe rims. Cover with plastic wrap directly on surface to prevent skin from forming. Chill until cool. Remove plastic wrap. Cover with tight-fitting lids. Store in refrigerator for up to 1 week or in freezer for up to 3 months. Makes about 3 1/2 cups (875 mL).

1 tbsp. (15 mL): 35 Calories; 2 g Total Fat (0.5 g Mono, 0 g Poly, 1 g Sat); 20 mg Cholesterol; 4 g Carbohydrate; 0 g Fibre; trace Protein; 15 mg Sodium

Honeyed Pear Butter

Thick, smooth and sweet—this is an absolutely lovely combination of honey and pears. Plus it spreads perfectly on toast or muffins.

Chopped peeled pear (see Tip, page 14)	6 cups	1.5 L
Orange (or apple) juice	1/4 cup	60 mL
Bottled lemon juice	2 tbsp.	30 mL
Liquid honey	3/4 cup	175 mL
Orange liqueur	2 tsp.	10 mL
Vanilla bean	1/2	1/2
Salt, sprinkle		

Combine first 3 ingredients in Dutch oven. Bring to a boil. Reduce heat to medium. Cook, uncovered, for about 10 minutes, stirring occasionally, until pear is tender. Carefully process in batches in blender or food processor until smooth (see Safety Tip). Return to same pot.

Add remaining 4 ingredients. Stir. Bring to a boil on medium. Boil gently, uncovered, for 30 minutes, stirring often. Boil gently, partially covered, for about 15 minutes, stirring often, until thickened to a spreadable consistency. Remove from heat. Remove and discard vanilla bean. Fill 4 hot sterile 1/2 cup (125 mL) jars to within 1/4 inch (6 mm) of top. Remove air bubbles and adjust headspace if necessary. Wipe rims. Place hot metal lids on jars and screw on metal bands fingertip tight. Do not over-tighten. Process in boiling water bath for 15 minutes (see page 9). Remove jars. Let stand at room temperature until cool. Makes about 2 cups (500 mL).

1 tbsp. (15 mL): 40 Calories; 0 g Total Fat (0 g Mono, 0 g Poly, 0 g Sat); 0 mg Cholesterol; 11 g Carbohydrate; trace Fibre; 0 g Protein; 0 mg Sodium

Pictured on page 18.

Safety Tip: Follow manufacturer's instructions for processing hot liquids.

Gingered Apricot Orange Butter

You certainly won't find any dairy products in this butter—though it's lovely on toast like traditional butter! This delightful apricot preserve uses dried apricot so you can make it any time of year.

Chopped dried apricot	3 cups	750 mL
Orange juice	1 1/2 cups	375 mL
Water	1 1/2 cups	375 mL
Finely grated ginger root (or 3/4 tsp., 4 mL, ground ginger)	1 tbsp.	15 mL
Granulated sugar	2 cups	500 mL
Bottled lemon juice	1/2 cup	125 mL
Grated orange zest (see Tip, page 31)	2 tsp.	10 mL

Combine first 4 ingredients in large saucepan. Bring to a boil. Reduce heat to medium-low. Simmer, covered, for about 25 minutes until apricot is softened. Carefully process in blender or food processor until smooth (see Safety Tip). Return to same saucepan.

Add remaining 3 ingredients. Stir. Bring to a boil. Reduce heat to medium-low. Simmer, uncovered, for about 45 minutes, stirring often, until thickened to a spreadable consistency. Fill 4 hot sterile 1 cup (250 mL) jars to within 1/4 inch (6 mm) of top. Remove air bubbles and adjust headspace if necessary. Wipe rims. Place hot metal lids on jars and screw on metal bands fingertip tight. Do not over-tighten. Process in boiling water bath for 15 minutes (see page 9). Remove jars. Let stand at room temperature until cool. Makes about 4 cups (1 L).

1 tbsp. (15 mL): 45 Calories; 0 g Total Fat (0 g Mono, 0 g Poly, 0 g Sat); 0 mg Cholesterol; 11 g Carbohydrate; 0 g Fibre; 0 g Protein; 0 mg Sodium

Safety Tip: Follow manufacturer's instructions for processing hot liquids.

Maple Apple Butter

This smooth, spreadable butter combines the classic flavours of apple, maple and spice for a lovely topping on toast, bagels, muffins, pancakes or French toast.

Chopped peeled tart apple, such as Granny Smith (see Tip, below)	6 cups	1.5 L
Apple juice	3/4 cup	175 mL
Apple cider vinegar	2 tbsp.	30 mL
Cinnamon stick (4 inches, 10 cm)	1	1
Maple syrup	1/3 cup	75 mL
Brown sugar, packed	1/4 cup	60 mL
Salt, sprinkle		

Combine first 4 ingredients in Dutch oven. Bring to a boil. Reduce heat to medium. Cook, uncovered, for about 20 minutes, stirring occasionally, until apple is tender. Remove from heat. Remove and discard cinnamon stick. Carefully process in food processor until smooth (see Safety Tip). Return to same pot.

Add remaining 3 ingredients. Stir. Bring to a boil on medium. Boil gently, uncovered, for about 10 minutes, stirring constantly, until thickened to a spreadable consistency. Fill 4 hot sterile 1/2 cup (125 mL) jars to within 1/4 inch (6 mm) of top. Remove air bubbles and adjust headspace if necessary. Wipe rims. Place hot metal lids on jars and screw on metal bands fingertip tight. Do not over-tighten. Process in boiling water bath for 15 minutes (see page 9). Remove jars. Let stand at room temperature until cool. Makes about 2 cups (500 mL).

1 tbsp. (15 mL): 25 Calories; 0 g Total Fat (0 g Mono, 0 g Poly, 0 g Sat); 0 mg Cholesterol; 6 g Carbohydrate; 0 g Fibre; 0 g Protein; 0 mg Sodium

Safety Tip: Follow manufacturer's instructions for processing hot liquids.

 tip To prevent cut fresh fruit (like apples and pears) from turning brown, mix 1/4 cup (60 mL) lemon juice with 4 cups (1 L) water in a large bowl. As you're cutting the fruit, add it to the lemon juice mixture.

Mango Citrus Curd

Make use of convenient frozen mango, which has been harvested at its prime so the flavour's sure to be amazing! This curd can be used in cakes and trifles, or as a topping for biscuits and muffins.

Frozen mango pieces, thawed (with juice)	4 cups	1 L
Granulated sugar	3/4 cup	175 mL
Butter (or hard margarine), cut up	1/2 cup	125 mL
Lime juice	3 tbsp.	45 mL
Orange juice	2 tbsp.	30 mL
Salt	1/8 tsp.	0.5 mL
Egg yolks (large)	5	5
Grated lime zest (see Tip, page 31)	1/2 tsp.	2 mL
Grated orange zest (see Tip, page 31)	1/2 tsp.	2 mL

Process mango in food processor until smooth. Transfer to medium saucepan.

Add next 5 ingredients. Heat and stir on medium for about 5 minutes until sugar is dissolved and butter is melted. Remove from heat.

Beat egg yolks in medium heatproof bowl until frothy. Slowly add mango mixture, stirring constantly. Return to same pot. Heat and stir on medium for about 5 minutes until mixture is thick enough to coat back of a spoon. Do not boil. Strain through sieve into small bowl. Discard solids.

Add lime and orange zest. Stir. Fill clean plastic containers to within 1/2 inch (12 mm) of top (see Tip, page 79). Wipe rims. Cover with plastic wrap directly on surface to prevent skin from forming. Chill until cool. Remove plastic wrap. Cover with tight-fitting lids. Store in refrigerator for up to 1 week or in freezer for up to 3 months. Makes about 3 1/2 cups (875 mL).

1 tbsp. (15 mL): 35 Calories; 2 g Total Fat (0.5 g Mono, 0 g Poly, 1 g Sat); 20 mg Cholesterol; 5 g Carbohydrate; 0 g Fibre; 0 g Protein; 15 mg Sodium

Pictured on page 17.

Raspberry Curd

Enjoy the fresh summery flavour of raspberries in this creamy-textured curd. Perfect with angel's food cake or scones, or even spread on toast.

Fresh (or frozen, thawed) raspberries	3 cups	750 mL
Bottled lemon juice	1/2 cup	125 mL
Granulated sugar	1 cup	250 mL
Butter (or hard margarine), cut up	1/2 cup	125 mL
Large eggs	6	6

Process raspberries and lemon juice in blender or food processor until smooth. Strain through fine sieve into small bowl. Discard solids. Measure 2 cups (500 mL) juice into medium saucepan.

Add sugar and butter. Heat and stir on medium for about 5 minutes until sugar is dissolved and butter is melted. Remove from heat.

Beat eggs in medium heatproof bowl until frothy. Slowly add raspberry mixture, stirring constantly. Return to same pot. Heat and stir on medium for about 5 minutes until mixture is thick enough to coat back of a spoon. Do not boil. Strain through sieve into medium bowl. Discard solids. Fill clean plastic containers to within 1/2 inch (12 mm) of top (see Tip, page 79). Wipe rims. Cover with plastic wrap directly on surface to prevent skin from forming. Chill until cool. Remove plastic wrap. Cover with tight-fitting lids. Store in refrigerator for up to 1 week or in freezer for up to 3 months. Makes about 4 cups (1 L).

1 tbsp. (15 mL): 30 Calories; 1.5 g Total Fat (0.5 g Mono, 0 g Poly, 1 g Sat); 15 mg Cholesterol; 4 g Carbohydrate; 0 g Fibre; 0 g Protein; 15 mg Sodium

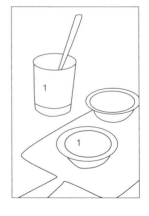

1. Mango Citrus Curd, page 15

Spiced Date Butter

This smooth spread gets its pleasing crunch from dates and packs a hint of exotic spices from cinnamon and cardamom. A great filling for pastries or cookie sandwiches, but it's also great on toast!

Chopped pitted dates	3 cups	750 mL
Chopped peeled cooking apple (such as McIntosh)	2 cups	500 mL
Bottled lemon juice	1/2 cup	125 mL
Water	1/2 cup	125 mL
Ground cinnamon	1 tsp.	5 mL
Ground cardamom	1/2 tsp.	2 mL
Ground cloves	1/8 tsp.	0.5 mL
Liquid honey	1/2 cup	125 mL

Combine first 7 ingredients in large saucepan. Bring to a boil. Reduce heat to medium. Cook, uncovered, for about 10 minutes, stirring occasionally, until dates are soft. Remove from heat. Transfer to food processor.

Add honey. Carefully process until smooth (see Safety Tip). Fill 6 hot sterile 1/2 cup (125 mL) jars to within 1/4 inch (6 mm) of top. Remove air bubbles and adjust headspace if necessary. Wipe rims. Place hot metal lids on jars and screw on metal bands fingertip tight. Do not over-tighten. Process in boiling water bath for 15 minutes (see page 9). Remove jars. Let stand at room temperature until cool. Makes about 3 cups (750 mL).

1 tbsp. (15 mL): 40 Calories; 0 g Total Fat (0 g Mono, 0 g Poly, 0 g Sat); 0 mg Cholesterol; 11 g Carbohydrate; trace Fibre; 0 g Protein; 0 mg Sodium

Safety Tip: Follow manufacturer's instructions for processing hot liquids.

1. Honeyed Pear Butter, page 12
2. Chili Peach Butter, page 21

Lively Limon Curd

Liven things up with the help of this creamy lemon-lime curd. Perfect for filling baked tart shells, or use as a filling for cakes. You may also fold this into sweetened whipped cream as an alternative to traditional cake frostings.

Granulated sugar	1 cup	250 mL
Butter (or hard margarine), cut up	1/3 cup	75 mL
Lime juice	1/3 cup	75 mL
Bottled lemon juice	3 tbsp.	45 mL
Grated lime zest (see Tip, page 31)	2 tsp.	10 mL
Large eggs	4	4

Combine first 5 ingredients in medium saucepan. Heat and stir on medium for about 3 minutes until sugar is dissolved and butter is melted. Remove from heat.

Beat eggs in medium heatproof bowl until frothy. Slowly add lime mixture, stirring constantly. Return to saucepan. Heat and stir on medium for about 3 minutes until mixture is thick enough to coat back of a spoon. Do not boil. Strain through sieve into small bowl. Discard solids. Fill clean plastic containers to within 1/2 inch (12 mm) of top (see Tip, page 79). Wipe rims. Cover with plastic wrap directly on surface to prevent skin from forming. Chill until cool. Remove plastic wrap. Cover with tight-fitting lids. Store in refrigerator for up to 1 week or in freezer for up to 3 months. Makes about 2 cups (500 mL).

1 tbsp. (15 mL): 45 Calories; 2.5 g Total Fat (0.5 g Mono, 0 g Poly, 1.5 g Sat); 20 mg Cholesterol; 6 g Carbohydrate; 0 g Fibre; trace Protein; 20 mg Sodium

Butters & Curds

Chili Peach Butter

Enjoy intense peach flavour with a subtle chili heat in this unique butter. Goes great with crepes, scones and pancakes, or use as a filling for pastries.

Chopped peeled peach (see Tip, page 129), about 12 peaches	8 cups	2 L
Bottled lemon juice	1/2 cup	125 mL
Granulated sugar	2 cups	500 mL
Dried crushed chilies	1 1/2 tsp.	7 mL

Combine peach and lemon juice in Dutch oven. Bring to a boil. Reduce heat to medium. Cook, uncovered, for about 10 minutes, stirring occasionally, until peach is tender. Carefully process in batches in blender or food processor until smooth (see Safety Tip). Return to same pot.

Add sugar. Stir. Bring to a boil on medium. Boil gently, uncovered, for about 50 minutes, stirring often, until thickened to a spreadable consistency.

Stir in chilies. Fill 6 hot sterile 1/2 cup (125 mL) jars to within 1/4 inch (6 mm) of top. Remove air bubbles and adjust headspace if necessary. Wipe rims. Place hot metal lids on jars and screw on metal bands fingertip tight. Do not over-tighten. Process in boiling water bath for 15 minutes (see page 9). Remove jars. Let stand at room temperature until cool. Makes about 2 2/3 cups (650 mL).

1 tbsp. (15 mL): 45 Calories; 0 g Total Fat (0 g Mono, 0 g Poly, 0 g Sat); 0 mg Cholesterol; 12 g Carbohydrate; 0 g Fibre; 0 g Protein; 0 mg Sodium

Pictured on page 18.

Safety Tip: Follow manufacturer's instructions for processing hot liquids.

Silky Onion Chutney

This smooth, flavourful chutney makes the perfect dipping sauce for samosas or pakoras. Also a good condiment for serving alongside grilled fish, poultry or pork.

Chopped onion	6 cups	1.5 L
Brown sugar, packed	1/2 cup	125 mL
Finely grated ginger root	2 tbsp.	30 mL
(or 1 1/2 tsp., 7 mL, ground)		
Garlic cloves, minced	4	4
Curry powder	1 tbsp.	15 mL
Cumin seed	2 tsp.	10 mL
Coarse (pickling) salt	1 tsp.	5 mL
Dried crushed chilies	1 tsp.	5 mL
Apple cider vinegar	1 cup	250 mL
Pineapple juice	1 cup	250 mL

Process 3 cups (750 mL) onion in blender or food processor until smooth. Transfer to large saucepan. Add remaining onion.

Add next 7 ingredients. Stir. Bring to a boil. Reduce heat to medium. Cook, uncovered, for about 30 minutes, stirring often, until onion is tender.

Add vinegar and pineapple juice. Bring to a boil, stirring occasionally. Reduce heat to medium. Boil gently, uncovered, for about 15 minutes, stirring often, until thickened. Fill 5 hot sterile 1/2 cup (125 mL) jars to within 1/2 inch (12 mm) of top. Remove air bubbles and adjust headspace if necessary. Wipe rims. Place hot metal lids on jars and screw on metal bands fingertip tight. Do not over-tighten. Process in boiling water bath for 15 minutes (see page 9). Remove jars. Let stand at room temperature until cool. Makes about 2 1/4 cups (550 mL).

1 tbsp. (15 mL): 25 Calories; 0 g Total Fat (0 g Mono, 0 g Poly, 0 g Sat); 0 mg Cholesterol; 6 g Carbohydrate; 0 g Fibre; 0 g Protein; 65 mg Sodium

Smoky Pear Salsa

This combination of sweet pear with smoky chipotle peppers makes a great topping for pan-seared catfish or chicken quesadillas. Serve with a frosty margarita to complete the experience!

Chopped red onion	1 cup	250 mL
Chopped red pepper	1 cup	250 mL
Apple cider vinegar	1/2 cup	125 mL
Granulated sugar	1/2 cup	125 mL
Chopped chipotle peppers in adobo sauce (see Tip, page 94)	1 tbsp.	15 mL
Salt	1 tsp.	5 mL
Ground cumin	1/2 tsp.	2 mL
Turmeric	1/2 tsp.	2 mL
Chopped peeled pear (see Tip, page 14)	4 cups	1 L

Combine first 8 ingredients in large saucepan. Bring to a boil. Reduce heat to medium. Cook, uncovered, for about 10 minutes, stirring often, until liquid is reduced.

Add pear. Heat and stir for about 1 minute until heated through. Fill 4 hot sterile 1 cup (250 mL) jars to within 1/2 inch (12 mm) of top. Remove air bubbles and adjust headspace if necessary. Wipe rims. Place hot metal lids on jars and screw on metal bands fingertip tight. Do not over-tighten. Process in boiling water bath for 15 minutes (see page 9). Remove jars. Let stand at room temperature until cool. Makes about 4 cups (1 L).

1/4 cup (60 mL): 60 Calories; 1 g Total Fat (0 g Mono, 0 g Poly, 0 g Sat); 0 mg Cholesterol; 15 g Carbohydrate; 2 g Fibre; 0 g Protein; 150 mg Sodium

Pictured on page 53.

Pear and Plum Chutney

Sweet bites of pear and plum are featured in this pleasant chutney flavoured with chai spices. Delicious with soft cheeses such as brie, or served as a condiment with roast pork.

Chopped peeled pear (see Tip, page 14)	4 cups	1 L
Brown sugar, packed	2 cups	500 mL
Malt vinegar	2 cups	500 mL
Chopped black (or red) plums	1 1/2 cups	375 mL
Chopped red onion	1 cup	250 mL
Chopped red pepper	1/2 cup	125 mL
Minced crystallized ginger	1/3 cup	75 mL
Dried currants (or dark raisins)	1/4 cup	60 mL
Ground cinnamon	1 tsp.	5 mL
Ground cardamom	1/2 tsp.	2 mL
Ground ginger	1/2 tsp.	2 mL
Salt	1/2 tsp.	2 mL
Pepper	1/2 tsp.	2 mL

Combine all 13 ingredients in large saucepan. Bring to a boil, stirring constantly. Reduce heat to medium. Cook, uncovered, for about 30 minutes, stirring often, until thickened. Fill 5 hot sterile 1 cup (250 mL) jars to within 1/2 inch (12 mm) of top. Remove air bubbles and adjust headspace if necessary. Wipe rims. Place hot metal lids on jars and screw on metal bands fingertip tight. Do not over-tighten. Process in boiling water bath for 20 minutes (see page 9). Remove jars. Let stand at room temperature until cool. Makes about 5 cups (1.25 L).

1 tbsp. (15 mL): 30 Calories; 0 g Total Fat (0 g Mono, 0 g Poly, 0 g Sat); 0 mg Cholesterol; 8 g Carbohydrate; 0 g Fibre; 0 g Protein; 15 mg Sodium

Honey Corn Relish

A colourful corn relish that's both sweet and spicy. Honey, mustard and chilies are behind this delightful flavour combination. A versatile condiment that can be made with either fresh or frozen corn.

Apple cider vinegar	2 cups	500 mL
Liquid honey	2/3 cup	150 mL
Granulated sugar	1/3 cup	75 mL
Dry mustard	2 tsp.	10 mL
Celery seed	1 1/2 tsp.	7 mL
Salt	1 1/2 tsp.	7 mL
Turmeric	1/2 tsp.	2 mL
Dried crushed chilies	1/4 tsp.	1 mL
Fresh (or frozen, thawed) kernel corn	4 cups	1 L
Finely chopped red onion	1 cup	250 mL
Finely chopped celery	1/2 cup	125 mL
All-purpose flour	3 tbsp.	45 mL
Cold water	3 tbsp.	45 mL
Finely chopped zucchini (with peel)	1 cup	250 mL
Finely chopped red pepper	1/2 cup	125 mL

Combine first 8 ingredients in large saucepan. Bring to a boil, stirring occasionally.

Add next 3 ingredients. Stir. Reduce heat to medium. Boil gently, uncovered, for about 20 minutes, stirring often, until corn and celery are tender.

Whisk flour into water in small bowl until smooth. Add to corn mixture.

Add zucchini and red pepper. Stir. Bring to a boil. Heat and stir for about 5 minutes until thickened. Fill 6 hot sterile 1 cup (250 mL) jars to within 1/2 inch (12 mm) of top. Remove air bubbles and adjust headspace if necessary. Wipe rims. Place hot metal lids on jars and screw on metal bands fingertip tight. Do not over-tighten. Process in boiling water bath for 20 minutes (see page 9). Remove jars. Let stand at room temperature until cool. Makes about 6 cups (1.5 L).

1 tbsp. (15 mL): 15 Calories; 0 g Total Fat (0 g Mono, 0 g Poly, 0 g Sat); 0 mg Cholesterol; 4 g Carbohydrate; 0 g Fibre; 0 g Protein; 35 mg Sodium

Mango Pineapple Salsa

Trade up those usual salsas for this sweet and spicy blend. The flavours of mango, pineapple and curry really increase the wow factor. Serve alongside grilled chicken or fish, or with tortilla chips for dipping.

Chopped peeled and seeded tomato (see Tip, page 129)	4 cups	1 L
Chopped ripe mango	3 cups	750 mL
Chopped fresh pineapple	1 1/2 cups	375 mL
Finely chopped red pepper	3/4 cup	175 mL
Finely chopped red onion	1/2 cup	125 mL
Mild (or hot) curry paste	1 tbsp.	15 mL
Dried crushed chilies	1/2 tsp.	2 mL
Brown sugar, packed	1/3 cup	75 mL
Apple cider vinegar	1/4 cup	60 mL
Bottled lemon juice	1/4 cup	60 mL
Finely chopped fresh cilantro	1/4 cup	60 mL
Finely chopped fresh mint	2 tbsp.	30 mL
Coarse (pickling) salt	1/2 tsp.	2 mL

Combine first 7 ingredients in Dutch oven. Bring to a boil, stirring constantly. Reduce heat to medium.

Add remaining 6 ingredients. Stir. Cook, uncovered, for about 15 minutes, stirring often, until slightly thickened. Fill 7 hot sterile 1 cup (250 mL) jars to within 1/2 inch (12 mm) of top. Remove air bubbles and adjust headspace if necessary. Wipe rims. Place hot metal lids on jars and screw on metal bands fingertip tight. Do not over-tighten. Process in boiling water bath for 25 minutes (see page 9). Remove jars. Let stand at room temperature until cool. Makes about 7 cups (1.75 L).

1/4 cup (60 mL): 35 Calories; 0 g Total Fat (0 g Mono, 0 g Poly, 0 g Sat); 0 mg Cholesterol; 8 g Carbohydrate; trace Fibre; 0 g Protein; 50 mg Sodium

Jazzy Sweet Pickle Relish

A bright and cheery relish with crunchy texture and sweet flavour. A mild jalapeño kick adds interest to this otherwise traditional sweet pickle relish. Perfect for serving on hot dogs and hamburgers.

Coarsely chopped trimmed pickling cucumbers	4 cups	1 L
Coarsely chopped onion	2 cups	500 mL
Coarsely chopped red pepper	2 cups	500 mL
Coarsely chopped yellow pepper	2 cups	500 mL
Chopped fresh jalapeño pepper (see Tip, page 116)	3 tbsp.	45 mL
Coarse (pickling) salt	2 tbsp.	30 mL
White vinegar	1 1/2 cups	375 mL
Granulated sugar	1 cup	250 mL
Celery seed	2 tsp.	10 mL
Mustard seed	2 tsp.	10 mL

Combine first 5 ingredients in large bowl. Process in batches in food processor with on/off motion, scraping down sides several times, until vegetables are finely chopped. Vegetable pieces should be about 1/8 inch (3 mm). Transfer to separate large bowl.

Sprinkle with salt. Mix well. Chill, covered, for at least 6 hours or overnight. Drain. Rinse with cold water. Drain well. Squeeze cucumber mixture to remove excess moisture.

Combine remaining 4 ingredients in large saucepan or Dutch oven. Bring to a boil, stirring occasionally. Reduce heat to medium. Boil gently, uncovered, for about 15 minutes, stirring occasionally, until slightly thickened. Add cucumber mixture. Cook for about 5 minutes, stirring often, until mixture is hot. Fill 4 hot sterile 1 cup (250 mL) jars to within 1/2 inch (12 mm) of top. Remove air bubbles and adjust headspace if necessary. Wipe rims. Place hot metal lids on jars and screw on metal bands fingertip tight. Do not over-tighten. Process in boiling water bath for 15 minutes (see page 9). Remove jars. Let stand at room temperature until cool. Makes about 4 cups (1 L).

1 tbsp. (15 mL): 30 Calories; 0 g Total Fat (0 g Mono, 0 g Poly, 0 g Sat); 0 mg Cholesterol; 7 g Carbohydrate; 0 g Fibre; 0 g Protein; 300 mg Sodium

Cherry Rhubarb Chutney

Cherry and rhubarb shouldn't be limited to pie fillings. This lovely spiced chutney features sweet cherries and tangy rhubarb in a picture-perfect condiment for chicken, pork or duck. Also good in cheese sandwiches or with crackers.

Chopped sweet cherries	6 cups	1.5 L
Diced fresh (or frozen) rhubarb	3 cups	750 mL
Chopped onion	1 1/2 cups	375 mL
Dried cranberries	1 1/2 cups	375 mL
Red wine vinegar	1 1/4 cups	300 mL
Chopped peeled tart apple, such as Granny Smith (see Tip, page 14)	1 cup	250 mL
Granulated sugar	1/2 cup	125 mL
Garlic cloves, minced (or 1/2 tsp., 2 mL, powder)	2	2
Ground ginger	1 tsp.	5 mL
Ground cinnamon	1/2 tsp.	2 mL
Salt	1/2 tsp.	2 mL
Pepper	1/2 tsp.	2 mL

Combine all 12 ingredients in Dutch oven. Bring to a boil, stirring occasionally. Reduce heat to medium. Cook, uncovered, for about 25 minutes, stirring often, until thickened. Fill 7 hot sterile 1 cup (250 mL) jars to within 1/2 inch (12 mm) of top. Remove air bubbles and adjust headspace if necessary. Wipe rims. Place hot metal lids on jars and screw on metal bands fingertip tight. Do not over-tighten. Process in boiling water bath for 15 minutes (see page 9). Remove jars. Let stand at room temperature until cool. Makes about 7 cups (1.75 L).

1 tbsp. (15 mL): 15 Calories; 0 g Total Fat (0 g Mono, 0 g Poly, 0 g Sat); 0 mg Cholesterol; 3 g Carbohydrate; 0 g Fibre; 0 g Protein; 10 mg Sodium

Zucchini Green Tomato Relish

A great way to use up your garden's bounty of zucchini and green tomatoes. This relish is perfect for hot dogs and hamburgers. Use a food processor to make quick work of chopping the vegetables.

Finely chopped zucchini (with peel)	3 cups	750 mL
Finely chopped green tomato	2 cups	500 mL
Finely chopped yellow pepper	1 1/2 cups	375 mL
Finely chopped onion	1 cup	250 mL
Coarse (pickling) salt	1/3 cup	75 mL
Ice cubes	4 cups	1 L
Granulated sugar	1 1/2 cups	375 mL
White vinegar	1 1/2 cups	375 mL
Mixed pickling spice, tied in double layer of cheesecloth	1 tbsp.	15 mL
Garlic cloves, minced (or 1/2 tsp., 2 mL, powder)	2	2
Turmeric	1/2 tsp.	2 mL
Ground allspice	1/4 tsp.	1 mL

Toss first 5 ingredients in large bowl. Scatter ice cubes over top. Let stand, covered, at room temperature for 3 hours. Drain. Rinse with cold water. Drain well.

Combine remaining 6 ingredients in Dutch oven. Bring to a boil, stirring occasionally. Add zucchini mixture. Stir. Reduce heat to medium. Cook, uncovered, for 20 minutes, stirring occasionally. Remove and discard cheesecloth bag. Fill 4 hot sterile 1 cup (250 mL) jars to within 1/2 inch (12 mm) of top. Remove air bubbles and adjust headspace if necessary. Wipe rims. Place hot metal lids on jars and screw on metal bands fingertip tight. Do not over-tighten. Process in boiling water bath for 15 minutes (see page 9). Remove jars. Let stand at room temperature until cool. Makes about 4 1/2 cups (1.1 L).

1 tbsp. (15 mL): 20 Calories; 0 g Total Fat (0 g Mono, 0 g Poly, 0 g Sat); 0 mg Cholesterol; 5 g Carbohydrate; 0 g Fibre; 0 g Protein; 500 mg Sodium

Mango Mint Chutney

This vibrant mango chutney boasts plenty of herb flavour and a mild dose of chili heat. Serve this traditional-style Indian chutney with lamb or chicken, and use fresh mango for best flavour.

Finely chopped ripe mango	3 1/2 cups	875 mL
Finely chopped fresh mint	1/4 cup	60 mL
Finely chopped fresh cilantro (or parsley)	3 tbsp.	45 mL
Finely chopped onion	3 tbsp.	45 mL
Lime juice	1 tbsp.	15 mL
Finely diced fresh hot chili pepper (see Tip, page 116)	2 tsp.	10 mL
Garlic clove, minced (or 1/4 tsp., 1 mL, powder)	1	1
Grated lime zest (see Tip, page 31)	1 tsp.	5 mL
Salt	1/2 tsp.	2 mL
Coarsely ground pepper	1/4 tsp.	1 mL
Cumin seed, crushed	1/8 tsp.	0.5 mL

Combine all 11 ingredients in large bowl. Chill, covered, for 1 hour. Fill clean plastic containers to within 1/2 inch (12 mm) of top (see Tip, page 79). Wipe rims. Cover with tight-fitting lids. Store in refrigerator for up to 3 days or in freezer for up to 6 months. Makes about 3 1/2 cups (875 mL).

1 tbsp. (15 mL): 5 Calories; 0 g Total Fat (0 g Mono, 0 g Poly, 0 g Sat); 0 mg Cholesterol; 2 g Carbohydrate; 0 g Fibre; 0 g Protein; 20 mg Sodium

Pictured on page 35.

Cucumber Corn Salsa

This sweet corn salsa is filled with crisp, colourful vegetables. A very appealing topping for tacos or tortilla chips.

Cooking oil	2 tsp.	10 mL
Fresh (or frozen, thawed) kernel corn	1 1/2 cups	375 mL
Finely chopped onion	1 cup	250 mL
Diced peeled English cucumber	1 1/2 cups	375 mL
Diced red pepper	1 cup	250 mL
Chopped fresh parsley	1/4 cup	60 mL
White wine vinegar	3 tbsp.	45 mL
Diced fresh hot chili pepper (see Tip, page 116)	1 tbsp.	15 mL
Granulated sugar	1 tsp.	5 mL
Salt	1/2 tsp.	2 mL

Heat cooking oil in large frying pan on medium. Add corn and onion. Cook for about 8 minutes, stirring often, until onion is softened.

Combine remaining 7 ingredients in large bowl. Add corn mixture. Stir. Let stand at room temperature until cool. Fill clean plastic containers to within 1/2 inch (12 mm) of top (see Tip, page 79). Wipe rims. Cover with tight-fitting lids. Store in refrigerator for up to 5 days or in freezer for up to 6 months. Makes about 2 2/3 cups (650 mL).

1/4 cup (60 mL): 40 Calories; 1 g Total Fat (0.5 g Mono, 0 g Poly, 0 g Sat); 0 mg Cholesterol; 7 g Carbohydrate; 1 g Fibre; trace Protein; 110 mg Sodium

 tip When a recipe calls for both grated zest and juice, it's easier to grate the fruit first, then juice it. Be careful not to grate down to the pith (white part of the peel), which is bitter and best avoided.

Piccalilli Relish

This lovely relish is a bit more sour than sweet. A nice hit of ginger hides in the background to add depth to the complex array of flavours in this inviting relish.

Finely chopped cabbage	2 cups	500 mL
Finely chopped English cucumber (with peel)	1 1/2 cups	375 mL
Finely chopped fresh (or frozen) green beans	1 cup	250 mL
Finely chopped onion	1 cup	250 mL
Finely chopped red pepper	1 cup	250 mL
Finely chopped yellow pepper	1 cup	250 mL
Salt	2 tbsp.	30 mL
White vinegar	1 1/2 cups	375 mL
Water	2/3 cup	150 mL
Granulated sugar	1/2 cup	125 mL
Finely grated ginger root (or 1 tsp., 5 mL, ground ginger)	2 tbsp.	30 mL
Mustard seed	4 tsp.	20 mL
Turmeric	1 tsp.	5 mL

Toss first 7 ingredients in large bowl. Let stand, covered, at room temperature for at least 8 hours or overnight. Drain. Rinse with cold water. Drain well. Squeeze cabbage mixture to remove excess moisture.

Combine remaining 6 ingredients in Dutch oven. Bring to a boil, stirring occasionally. Add cabbage mixture. Stir. Reduce heat to medium. Cook, uncovered, for 20 minutes, stirring occasionally. Fill 4 hot sterile 1 cup (250 mL) jars to within 1/2 inch (12 mm) of top. Remove air bubbles and adjust headspace if necessary. Wipe rims. Place hot metal lids on jars and screw on metal bands fingertip tight. Do not over-tighten. Process in boiling water bath for 15 minutes (see page 9). Remove jars. Let stand at room temperature until cool. Makes about 4 1/4 cups (1 L).

1 tbsp. (15 mL): 10 Calories; 0 g Total Fat (0 g Mono, 0 g Poly, 0 g Sat); 0 mg Cholesterol; 3 g Carbohydrate; 0 g Fibre; 0 g Protein; 210 mg Sodium

Roasted Grape Relish

This unique and unexpected relish makes a sophisticated addition to a holiday cheese platter, or a perfect topping for grilled seafood at a summer barbecue. A nice blend of sweet and sour flavours.

Seedless red grapes, halved	6 cups	1.5 L
Cooking oil	2 tbsp.	30 mL
Pepper	1/4 tsp.	1 mL
Finely chopped red onion	1 1/2 cups	375 mL
Red wine vinegar	1 cup	250 mL
Brown sugar, packed	3/4 cup	175 mL
Coarse (pickling) salt	1 tsp.	5 mL
Grated orange zest	1 tsp.	5 mL
Fennel seed, crushed (see Tip, below)	1/2 tsp.	2 mL

Toss first 3 ingredients in large bowl. Transfer to ungreased baking sheet. Bake in 400°F (205°C) oven for about 40 minutes, stirring occasionally, until grapes are shrivelled and starting to brown.

Combine remaining 6 ingredients in large saucepan. Bring to a boil. Reduce heat to medium-low. Simmer, uncovered, for about 15 minutes, stirring often, until reduced. Add grapes. Stir. Fill 3 hot sterile 1 cup (250 mL) jars to within 1/2 inch (12 mm) of top. Remove air bubbles and adjust headspace if necessary. Wipe rims. Place hot metal lids on jars and screw on metal bands fingertip tight. Do not over-tighten. Process in boiling water bath for 15 minutes (see page 9). Remove jars. Let stand at room temperature until cool. Makes about 3 1/3 cups (825 mL).

1 tbsp. (15 mL): 30 Calories; 0.5 g Total Fat (0 g Mono, 0 g Poly, 0 g Sat); 0 mg Cholesterol; 7 g Carbohydrate; 0 g Fibre; 0 g Protein; 45 mg Sodium

 tip   To crush fennel seed, place in large resealable freezer bag. Seal bag. Gently hit with flat side of meat mallet or with rolling pin.

Hot Tomato Garlic Chutney

If you really like to heat things up, this chutney might be just the thing. There's plenty of hot chilies in this cheerful mix that blends a nice array of otherwise sweet and tangy flavours.

Coarsely chopped seeded tomato	6 cups	1.5 L
Chopped onion	1 1/2 cups	375 mL
Diced peeled tart apple, such as Granny Smith (see Tip, page 14)	1 1/2 cups	375 mL
Granulated sugar	1 1/2 cups	375 mL
White wine vinegar	1 1/2 cups	375 mL
Sultana raisins	1 cup	250 mL
Finely diced fresh hot chili pepper (see Tip, page 116)	3 tbsp.	45 mL
Garlic cloves, minced	6	6
Coarse (pickling) salt	1 tbsp.	15 mL
Finely grated ginger root (or 1/2 tsp., 2 mL, ground ginger)	2 tsp.	10 mL
Fennel seed, crushed (see Tip, page 33)	1 tsp.	5 mL
Ground cinnamon	1/2 tsp.	2 mL
Ground cloves	1/4 tsp.	1 mL

Combine all 13 ingredients in Dutch oven. Bring to a boil, stirring often. Reduce heat to medium. Cook, uncovered, for about 1 hour, stirring often, until thickened. Fill 5 hot sterile 1 cup (250 mL) jars to within 1/2 inch (12 mm) of top. Remove air bubbles and adjust headspace if necessary. Wipe rims. Place hot metal lids on jars and screw on metal bands fingertip tight. Do not over-tighten. Process in boiling water bath for 15 minutes (see page 9). Remove jars. Let stand at room temperature until cool. Makes about 5 1/2 cups (1.4 L).

1 tbsp. (15 mL): 20 Calories; 0 g Total Fat (0 g Mono, 0 g Poly, 0 g Sat); 0 mg Cholesterol; 6 g Carbohydrate; 0 g Fibre; 0 g Protein; 75 mg Sodium

1. Mango Mint Chutney, page 30

Spiced Apple Chutney

Though this recipe may look like it could be spicy-hot, the spices are blended so perfectly that you'll simply notice a nicely spiced background to the sweet-tart blend of apples and cranberries.

Chopped unpeeled red apple (such as Spartan)	2 cups	500 mL
Chopped unpeeled tart apple (such as Granny Smith)	2 cups	500 mL
Chopped red onion	1 cup	250 mL
Dried cranberries	1 cup	250 mL
Apple cider vinegar	1/2 cup	125 mL
Granulated sugar	1/2 cup	125 mL
Ground ginger	1 tsp.	5 mL
Salt	1 tsp.	5 mL
Dried crushed chilies	1/2 tsp.	2 mL
Ground nutmeg	1/4 tsp.	1 mL

Combine all 10 ingredients in large saucepan. Bring to a boil, stirring often. Reduce heat to medium. Cook, uncovered, for about 10 minutes, stirring often, until slightly thickened. Fill 3 hot sterile 1 cup (250 mL) jars to within 1/2 inch (12 mm) of top. Remove air bubbles and adjust headspace if necessary. Wipe rims. Place hot metal lids on jars and screw on metal bands fingertip tight. Do not over-tighten. Process in boiling water bath for 15 minutes (see page 9). Remove jars. Let stand at room temperature until cool. Makes about 3 cups (750 mL).

1 tbsp. (15 mL): 20 Calories; 0 g Total Fat (0 g Mono, 0 g Poly, 0 g Sat); 0 mg Cholesterol; 5 g Carbohydrate; 0 g Fibre; 0 g Protein; 45 mg Sodium

1. Nectarine Plum Conserve, page 49

Dilly Borscht Relish

This fine-textured beet relish has a lovely deep red colour. Try it with roast beef or pork, or served on a bratwurst sausage or burger. You could even try it with sour cream to complete the borscht flavour experience!

Coarsely chopped peeled beet, about 1 lb., 454 g (see Tip, page 103)	3 cups	750 mL
Apple cider vinegar	1 1/4 cups	300 mL
Granulated sugar	2/3 cup	150 mL
Water	1/3 cup	75 mL
Coarse (pickling) salt	1 tsp.	5 mL
Dill seed	1 tsp.	5 mL
Mustard seed	1 tsp.	5 mL
Coarsely chopped red cabbage	1 1/2 cups	375 mL
Coarsely chopped carrot	1/2 cup	125 mL
Coarsely chopped celery	1/2 cup	125 mL
Coarsely chopped red onion	1/2 cup	125 mL
Tomato paste (see Tip, page 92)	1 tbsp.	15 mL
Chopped fresh dill	1 tbsp.	15 mL

Process beet in food processor until finely chopped.

Combine next 6 ingredients in large saucepan. Bring to a boil. Add beet. Stir. Reduce heat to medium-low. Simmer, covered, for about 15 minutes until beet is almost tender.

Process next 4 ingredients in food processor until finely chopped. Add to beet mixture. Add tomato paste. Stir. Simmer, uncovered, for about 15 minutes, stirring often, until vegetables are tender.

Add dill. Stir. Fill 4 hot sterile 1 cup (250 mL) jars to within 1/2 inch (12 mm) of top. Remove air bubbles and adjust headspace if necessary. Wipe rims. Place hot metal lids on jars and screw on metal bands fingertip tight. Do not over-tighten. Process in boiling water bath for 20 minutes (see page 9). Remove jars. Let stand at room temperature until cool. Makes about 4 cups (1 L).

1 tbsp. (15 mL): 15 Calories; 0 g Total Fat (0 g Mono, 0 g Poly, 0 g Sat); 0 mg Cholesterol; 3 g Carbohydrate; 0 g Fibre; 0 g Protein; 40 mg Sodium

Smokin' Freezer Salsa

This sweet salsa packs a nice punch of chili heat! Freezer salsa is so convenient and only takes a little while to defrost before you can enjoy it. Be sure to give the thawed salsa a quick stir before serving.

Cooking oil	1 tsp.	5 mL
Finely chopped onion	3/4 cup	175 mL
Finely chopped celery	1/2 cup	125 mL
Garlic cloves, minced	2	2
(or 1/2 tsp., 2 mL, powder)		
Tomato paste (see Tip, page 92)	1/4 cup	60 mL
Chopped peeled seeded tomato	5 cups	1.25 L
(see Tip, page 129)		
Diced red pepper	1 cup	250 mL
Can of diced green chilies	4 oz.	113 g
Lime juice	1/4 cup	60 mL
Chopped chipotle peppers in adobo sauce	2 tbsp.	30 mL
(see Tip, page 94)		
Granulated sugar	2 tbsp.	30 mL
Ground cumin	1 tsp.	5 mL
Salt	1/2 tsp.	2 mL
Chopped fresh cilantro (or parsley)	2 tbsp.	30 mL

Heat cooking oil in large saucepan or Dutch oven on medium. Add next 3 ingredients. Cook for about 5 minutes, stirring often, until onion and celery are softened.

Add tomato paste. Heat and stir for 1 minute.

Add next 8 ingredients. Stir. Bring to a boil. Reduce heat to medium-low. Cook, uncovered, for about 30 minutes, stirring occasionally, until thickened.

Add cilantro. Stir. Fill clean plastic containers to within 1/2 inch (12 mm) of top (see Tip, page 79). Wipe rims. Let stand until cool. Cover with tight-fitting lids. Store in refrigerator for up to 2 weeks or in freezer for up to 6 months. Makes about 5 cups (1.25 L).

1/4 cup (60 mL): 25 Calories; 1.5 g Total Fat (0 g Mono, 0 g Poly, 0 g Sat); 0 mg Cholesterol; 5 g Carbohydrate; 1 g Fibre; trace Protein; 105 mg Sodium

Peach Salsa

This fresh and fruity offering goes great with tortilla chips, but we also suggest you try serving it with grilled meats for a true taste of summer!

Chopped peeled peach (see Tip, page 129)	8 cups	2 L
Chopped red onion	2 cups	500 mL
Chopped red pepper	1 cup	250 mL
Red wine vinegar	3/4 cup	175 mL
Finely chopped fresh jalapeño pepper (see Tip, page 116)	2 tbsp.	30 mL
Lime juice	2 tbsp.	30 mL
Liquid honey	2 tbsp.	30 mL
Dried basil	2 tsp.	10 mL
Garlic cloves, minced (or 1/2 tsp., 2 mL, powder)	2	2
Coarse (pickling) salt	1 tsp.	5 mL
Ground cumin	1 tsp.	5 mL
Chopped fresh cilantro	1/4 cup	60 mL

Combine first 11 ingredients in Dutch oven. Bring to a boil, stirring often. Reduce heat to medium. Cook, uncovered, for 10 minutes, stirring occasionally.

Stir in cilantro. Fill 4 hot sterile 2 cup (500 mL) jars to within 1/2 inch (12 mm) of top. Remove air bubbles and adjust headspace if necessary. Wipe rims. Place hot metal lids on jars and screw on metal bands fingertip tight. Do not over-tighten. Process in boiling water bath for 25 minutes (see page 9). Remove jars. Let stand at room temperature until cool. Makes about 9 cups (2.25 L).

1/4 cup (60 mL): 25 Calories; 0 g Total Fat (0 g Mono, 0 g Poly, 0 g Sat); 0 mg Cholesterol; 6 g Carbohydrate; trace Fibre; trace Protein; 65 mg Sodium

Tomato Salsa

Sometimes simplicity is all you're looking for. This all-purpose tomato salsa has a moderate amount of chili heat with plenty of onions and peppers. The perfect topping for tacos, or use as a dip for tortilla chips.

Coarsely chopped seeded tomato (about 2 lbs., 900 g)	6 cups	1.5 L
Chopped onion	1 1/2 cups	375 mL
Chopped red pepper	1 cup	250 mL
Can of tomato paste	5 1/2 oz.	156 mL
Chopped green pepper	1/2 cup	125 mL
Finely chopped fresh jalapeño pepper (see Tip, page 116)	1/2 cup	125 mL
Finely chopped hot banana pepper (see Tip, page 116)	1/2 cup	125 mL
White vinegar	1/2 cup	125 mL
Lime juice	3 tbsp.	45 mL
Granulated sugar	4 tsp.	20 mL
Coarse (pickling) salt	2 tsp.	10 mL
Dried oregano	1 tsp.	5 mL
Garlic clove, minced (or 1/4 tsp., 1 mL, powder)	1	1
Ground cumin	1 tsp.	5 mL
Paprika	1 tsp.	5 mL

Combine all 15 ingredients in Dutch oven. Bring to a boil, stirring constantly. Reduce heat to medium. Cook, uncovered, for about 30 minutes, stirring often, until thickened. Fill 7 hot sterile 1 cup (250 mL) jars to within 1/2 inch (12 mm) of top. Remove air bubbles and adjust headspace if necessary. Wipe rims. Place hot metal lids on jars and screw on metal bands fingertip tight. Do not over-tighten. Process in boiling water bath for 25 minutes (see page 9). Remove jars. Let stand at room temperature until cool. Makes about 7 cups (1.75 L).

1/4 cup (60 mL): 20 Calories; 0 g Total Fat (0 g Mono, 0 g Poly, 0 g Sat); 0 mg Cholesterol; 5 g Carbohydrate; 1 g Fibre; trace Protein; 180 mg Sodium

Beet Cranberry Chutney

You'll certainly agree that spice is nice once you've tried this lovely chutney. A delicious blend of ginger, cinnamon, cloves and other spices add the perfect touch to this flavourful blend of beets and cranberries.

Chopped ginger root	2 tbsp.	30 mL
Whole black peppercorns	2 tsp.	10 mL
Whole allspice	1 tsp.	5 mL
Whole cloves	1/2 tsp.	2 mL
Whole green cardamom, bruised (see Note)	6	6
Diced peeled beet, about 1 lb., 454 g (see Tip, page 103)	3 cups	750 mL
Fresh (or frozen) cranberries	1 1/2 cups	375 mL
Chopped red onion	1 cup	250 mL
Malt vinegar	1 cup	250 mL
Brown sugar, packed	2/3 cup	150 mL
Chopped dried cranberries	1/2 cup	125 mL
Salt	1 tsp.	5 mL
Ground cardamom	1/2 tsp.	2 mL
Ground cinnamon	1/2 tsp.	2 mL

Place first 5 ingredients in centre of cheesecloth square. Draw up corners and tie with butcher's string.

Combine remaining 9 ingredients in large saucepan. Add cheesecloth bag. Bring to a boil on medium. Cook, covered, for about 20 minutes, stirring occasionally, until beet is tender. Reduce heat to medium-low. Simmer, uncovered, for about 5 minutes until thickened. Remove and discard cheesecloth bag. Fill 3 hot sterile 1 cup (250 mL) jars to within 1/2 inch (12 mm) of top. Remove air bubbles and adjust headspace if necessary. Wipe rims. Place hot metal lids on jars and screw on metal bands fingertip tight. Do not over-tighten. Process in boiling water bath for 15 minutes (see page 9). Remove jars. Let stand at room temperature until cool. Makes about 3 cups (750 mL).

1 tbsp. (15 mL): 20 Calories; 0 g Total Fat (0 g Mono, 0 g Poly, 0 g Sat); 0 mg Cholesterol; 5 g Carbohydrate; trace Fibre; 0 g Protein; 55 mg Sodium

Note: To bruise cardamom, pound pods with mallet or press with flat side of wide knife to "bruise" or crack them open slightly.

Salsa Verde

Salsa verde is a gently spiced, green-coloured salsa that features the distinctive flavour of tomatillos and green chilies. This version also includes a fun little taste of tequila! Deliciously tangy and not too spicy.

Chopped tomatillo, about 2 1/4 lbs., 1 kg (see Note)	6 cups	1.5 L
Chopped onion	1 1/2 cups	375 mL
Cans of diced green chilies (4 oz., 113 g, each)	2	2
Chopped green pepper	2/3 cup	150 mL
White vinegar	2/3 cup	150 mL
Lime juice	1/4 cup	60 mL
Granulated sugar	2 tbsp.	30 mL
Garlic cloves, minced (or 1/2 tsp., 2 mL, powder)	2	2
Coarse (pickling) salt	1 tsp.	5 mL
Dried oregano	1 tsp.	5 mL
Ground cumin	1 tsp.	5 mL
Dried crushed chilies	1/2 tsp.	2 mL
Chopped fresh cilantro	3 tbsp.	45 mL
Tequila (optional)	1/4 cup	60 mL

Combine first 12 ingredients in Dutch oven. Bring to a boil, stirring often. Reduce heat to medium. Cook, uncovered, for about 25 minutes, stirring occasionally, until reduced and slightly thickened.

Add cilantro and tequila. Stir. Fill 3 hot sterile 2 cup (500 mL) jars to within 1/2 inch (12 mm) of top. Remove air bubbles and adjust headspace if necessary. Wipe rims. Place hot metal lids on jars and screw on metal bands fingertip tight. Do not over-tighten. Process in boiling water bath for 20 minutes (see page 9). Remove jars. Let stand at room temperature until cool. Makes about 6 1/2 cups (1.6 L).

1/4 cup (60 mL): 20 Calories; 0 g Total Fat (0 g Mono, 0 g Poly, 0 g Sat); 0 mg Cholesterol; 5 g Carbohydrate; trace Fibre; trace Protein; 125 mg Sodium

Note: Tomatillos (pronounced tohm-ah-TEE-ohs) are similar in appearance to small, green tomatoes with papery husks that are removed before cooking. Tomatillos have a sour taste that mellows when cooked. Select tomatillos with tight husks and store them in a paper bag in the fridge. Tomatillos should be washed well before using.

Squashed Relish

This beautiful relish boasts finely diced bits of squash, zucchini and other colourful vegetables. Sweet, tangy and just a little bit spicy.

Finely chopped butternut squash	2 cups	500 mL
Finely chopped zucchini (with peel)	2 cups	500 mL
Coarse (pickling) salt	2 tbsp.	30 mL
Granulated sugar	1 1/4 cups	300 mL
Apple cider vinegar	1 cup	250 mL
Finely chopped onion	1 cup	250 mL
Finely chopped fresh jalapeño pepper (see Tip, page 116)	1/4 cup	60 mL
Celery seed	1 tsp.	5 mL
Mustard seed	1 tsp.	5 mL
Finely chopped red pepper	1 cup	250 mL

Toss first 3 ingredients in medium bowl. Let stand, covered, at room temperature for 1 hour. Drain. Rinse with cold water. Drain well. Squeeze squash mixture to remove excess moisture.

Combine next 6 ingredients in large saucepan. Bring to a boil, stirring occasionally.

Add red pepper and squash mixture. Stir. Reduce heat to medium. Cook, uncovered, for about 15 minutes until vegetables are tender-crisp. Fill 4 hot sterile 1 cup (250 mL) jars to within 1/2 inch (12 mm) of top. Remove air bubbles and adjust headspace if necessary. Wipe rims. Place hot metal lids on jars and screw on metal bands fingertip tight. Do not over-tighten. Process in boiling water bath for 15 minutes (see page 9). Remove jars. Let stand at room temperature until cool. Makes about 4 cups (1 L).

1 tbsp. (15 mL): 20 Calories; 0 g Total Fat (0 g Mono, 0 g Poly, 0 g Sat); 0 mg Cholesterol; 5 g Carbohydrate; 0 g Fibre; 0 g Protein; 210 mg Sodium

Eggplant Salsa

This is definitely not your average salsa. There's plenty going on in this flavourful blend of eggplant, tomato, zucchini and olives. Try it with pita crisps, tortilla chips or grilled meats.

Chopped eggplant (with peel), 1/2 inch, 12 mm, pieces (about 1 lb., 454 g)	4 cups	1 L
Coarse (pickling) salt	2 tbsp.	30 mL
Chopped seeded Roma (plum) tomato (about 1 3/4 lbs., 790 g)	3 cups	750 mL
Diced red pepper	1 cup	250 mL
Diced zucchini (with peel)	1 cup	250 mL
Red wine vinegar	1 cup	250 mL
Finely chopped onion	1/2 cup	125 mL
Chopped green olives	1/4 cup	60 mL
Granulated sugar	2 tbsp.	30 mL
Tomato paste (see Tip, page 92)	2 tbsp.	30 mL
Dried oregano	2 tsp.	10 mL
Garlic cloves, minced (or 1/2 tsp., 2 mL powder)	2	2
Pepper	1/4 tsp.	1 mL
Capers (optional)	2 tbsp.	30 mL

Toss eggplant and coarse salt in large bowl. Let stand, covered, at room temperature for 2 hours. Drain. Rinse with cold water. Drain well.

Combine remaining 12 ingredients in Dutch oven. Bring to a boil, stirring often. Add eggplant. Stir. Reduce heat to medium. Cook, uncovered, for about 30 minutes, stirring occasionally, until thickened. Fill 3 hot sterile 2 cup (500 mL) jars to within 1/2 inch (12 mm) of top. Remove air bubbles and adjust headspace if necessary. Wipe rims. Place hot metal lids on jars and screw on metal bands fingertip tight. Do not over-tighten. Process in boiling water bath for 25 minutes (see page 9). Remove jars. Let stand at room temperature until cool. Makes about 6 cups (1.5 L).

1/4 cup (60 mL): 20 Calories; 0 g Total Fat (0 g Mono, 0 g Poly, 0 g Sat); 0 mg Cholesterol; 4 g Carbohydrate; 1 g Fibre; trace Protein; 600 mg Sodium

Pictured on page 53.

Orange Carrot Conserve

This vibrant, cheerful conserve will add a touch of sunshine to even the darkest of days. Loaded with orange flavour, a whole lot of carrot colour and a bit of almond crunch, this conserve offers all the very best.

Finely chopped orange segments (see Tip, page 146)	2 cups	500 mL
Finely grated carrot	2 cups	500 mL
Finely chopped dried apricot	1/2 cup	125 mL
Bottled lemon juice	1/4 cup	60 mL
Orange juice	1/4 cup	60 mL
Box of pectin crystals	2 oz.	57 g
Granulated sugar	5 cups	1.25 L
Chopped slivered almonds, toasted (see Tip, page 50)	1 cup	250 mL
Grated orange zest (see Tip, page 31)	2 tsp.	10 mL

Stir first 6 ingredients in Dutch oven until pectin is dissolved. Bring to a boil, stirring constantly.

Add sugar. Bring to a hard boil, stirring constantly. Boil hard for 1 minute, stirring constantly.

Add almonds and orange zest. Stir. Remove from heat. Fill 6 hot sterile 1 cup (250 mL) jars to within 1/4 inch (6 mm) of top. Remove air bubbles and adjust headspace if necessary. Wipe rims. Place hot metal lids on jars and screw on metal bands fingertip tight. Do not over-tighten. Process in boiling water bath for 15 minutes (see page 9). Remove jars. Let stand at room temperature until cool. Makes about 6 1/2 cups (1.6 L).

1 tbsp. (15 mL): 50 Calories; 0.5 g Total Fat (0 g Mono, 0 g Poly, 0 g Sat); 0 mg Cholesterol; 11 g Carbohydrate; 0 g Fibre; 0 g Protein; 0 mg Sodium

Savoury Cranberry Compote

A nice balance of sweet and sour, soft and crunchy, and all with the option of adding a little heat. Serve with poultry, grilled fish or sandwiches.

Sliced red onion	2 cups	500 mL
Dried cranberries	1 cup	250 mL
Julienned carrot (see Tip, below)	1 cup	250 mL
Orange juice	1 cup	250 mL
Red wine vinegar	1/4 cup	60 mL
Finely grated ginger root	3 tbsp.	45 mL
(or 2 1/4 tsp., 11 mL, ground ginger)		
Garlic cloves, minced (or 3/4 tsp.,	3	3
4 mL, powder)		
Coarse (pickling) salt	1/2 tsp.	2 mL
Dried crushed chilies (optional)	1/2 tsp.	2 mL
Orange marmalade	1 cup	250 mL

Combine first 9 ingredients in large saucepan. Bring to a boil, stirring often. Reduce heat to medium. Boil gently, covered, for about 20 minutes, stirring occasionally, until onion is tender.

Add marmalade. Stir. Bring to a boil. Fill 3 hot sterile 1 cup (250 mL) jars to within 1/4 inch (6 mm) of top. Remove air bubbles and adjust headspace if necessary. Wipe rims. Place hot metal lids on jars and screw on metal bands fingertip tight. Do not over-tighten. Process in boiling water bath for 15 minutes (see page 9). Remove jars. Let stand at room temperature until cool. Makes about 3 1/2 cups (875 mL).

1 tbsp. (15 mL): 25 Calories; 0 g Total Fat (0 g Mono, 0 g Poly, 0 g Sat); 0 mg Cholesterol; 6 g Carbohydrate; 0 g Fibre; 0 g Protein; 25 mg Sodium

 tip To julienne, cut into very thin strips that resemble matchsticks.

Chocolate Cherry Preserves

This deep, dark and decadent mix of cherries, rhubarb and cocoa powder tastes just like chocolate-covered cherries and makes a great topping for ice cream, waffles, pancakes or French toast.

Coarsely chopped sweet cherries	2 cups	500 mL
Finely chopped fresh (or frozen) rhubarb	1 cup	250 mL
Water	1/2 cup	125 mL
Bottled lemon juice	3 tbsp.	45 mL
Granulated sugar	3 cups	750 mL
Cocoa, sifted if lumpy	3 tbsp.	45 mL
Cherry liqueur	3 tbsp.	45 mL

Combine first 4 ingredients in Dutch oven. Bring to a boil on medium. Boil gently, uncovered, for 5 minutes, stirring occasionally.

Combine sugar and cocoa in medium bowl. Add to cherry mixture. Heat and stir for about 5 minutes until mixture comes to a hard boil. Boil hard for about 12 minutes, stirring constantly, until mixture gels when tested on small cold plate (see Tip, page 77). Remove from heat.

Stir in liqueur. Fill 3 hot sterile 1 cup (250 mL) jars to within 1/4 inch (6 mm) of top. Remove air bubbles and adjust headspace if necessary. Wipe rims. Place hot metal lids on jars and screw on metal bands fingertip-tight. Do not over-tighten. Process in boiling water bath for 15 minutes (see page 9). Remove jars. Let stand at room temperature until cool. Makes about 3 cups (750 mL).

1 tbsp. (15 mL): 50 Calories; 0 g Total Fat (0 g Mono, 0 g Poly, 0 g Sat); 0 mg Cholesterol; 13 g Carbohydrate; 0 g Fibre; 0 g Protein; 0 mg Sodium

Nectarine Plum Conserve

Lovely colour and texture in this delightful conserve. Sweet fruit and nutty almond slivers complement each other so well. This conserve is free of spices, which allows the colours and flavours of the fruit to really shine.

Chopped black (or red) plums	1 1/2 cups	375 mL
Chopped unpeeled nectarine	1 1/2 cups	375 mL
Chopped dried apricot	1/2 cup	125 mL
Bottled lemon juice	1/4 cup	60 mL
Water	1/4 cup	60 mL
Box of pectin crystals	2 oz.	57 g
Granulated sugar	5 cups	1.25 L
Slivered almonds, toasted (see Tip, page 50)	1 cup	250 mL
Chopped red glazed cherries	1/2 cup	125 mL

Stir first 6 ingredients in Dutch oven until pectin is dissolved. Bring to a boil, stirring often.

Add sugar. Bring to a hard boil, stirring constantly. Boil hard for 1 minute, stirring constantly.

Add almonds and cherries. Stir. Remove from heat. Fill 6 hot sterile 1 cup (250 mL) jars to within 1/4 inch (6 mm) of top. Remove air bubbles and adjust headspace if necessary. Wipe rims. Place hot metal lids on jars and screw on metal bands fingertip tight. Do not over-tighten. Process in boiling water bath for 15 minutes (see page 9). Remove jars. Let stand at room temperature until cool. Makes about 6 cups (1.5 L).

1 tbsp. **(15 mL):** *50 Calories; 0.5 g Total Fat (0 g Mono, 0 g Poly, 0 g Sat); 0 mg Cholesterol; 13 g Carbohydrate; 0 g Fibre; 0 g Protein; 0 mg Sodium*

Pictured on page 36.

Blueberry Preserves

Beautiful purple-blue colour and delightfully sweet blueberry flavour. This sweet preserve is good on toast, pancakes or muffins, or as a topping for ice cream.

Granulated sugar	4 1/2 cups	1.1 L
Fresh (or frozen, thawed) blueberries	3 cups	750 mL
Fresh (or frozen, thawed) raspberries	1 cup	250 mL
Unsweetened apple juice	1/4 cup	60 mL
Raspberry vinegar	2 tbsp.	30 mL
Pouch of liquid pectin	3 oz.	85 mL

Combine first 5 ingredients in Dutch oven. Let stand for 1 hour. Bring to a hard boil, stirring constantly.

Add pectin. Boil hard for 1 minute, stirring constantly. Remove from heat. Skim and discard foam. Fill 5 hot sterile 1 cup (250 mL) jars to within 1/4 inch (6 mm) of top. Remove air bubbles and adjust headspace if necessary. Wipe rims. Place hot metal lids on jars and screw on metal bands fingertip tight. Do not over-tighten. Process in boiling water bath for 15 minutes (see page 9). Remove jars. Let stand at room temperature until cool. Makes about 5 1/2 cups (1.4 L).

1 tbsp. (15 mL): 40 Calories; 0 g Total Fat (0 g Mono, 0 g Poly, 0 g Sat); 0 mg Cholesterol; 11 g Carbohydrate; 0 g Fibre; 0 g Protein; 0 mg Sodium

 tip When toasting nuts, seeds or coconut, cooking times will vary for each type of nut—so never toast them together. For small amounts, place ingredient in an ungreased frying pan. Heat on medium for 3 to 5 minutes, stirring often, until golden. For larger amounts, spread ingredient evenly on an ungreased shallow pan. Bake in a 350°F (175°C) oven for 5 to 10 minutes, stirring or shaking often until golden.

Tropical Island Conserve

A sweet conserve with tropical flavours. Coconut adds a nice bit of texture.
Conserves are soft-textured jams that are often made without pectin, making
them a perfect spread or dessert sauce.

Diced ripe mango	2 cups	500 mL
Chopped orange segments	1 1/2 cups	375 mL
(see Tip, page 146), with juice		
Can of crushed pineapple, drained	19 oz.	540 mL
Bottled lemon juice	1/4 cup	60 mL
Grated lemon zest	1 tsp.	5 mL
Grated orange zest	1 tsp.	5 mL
Granulated sugar	5 cups	1.25 L
Flaked coconut	1 cup	250 mL
Chopped salted roasted macadamia nuts	1/2 cup	125 mL
White (light) rum	2 tbsp.	30 mL

Combine first 6 ingredients in Dutch oven. Bring to a boil, stirring
constantly.

Add sugar. Bring to a hard boil, stirring constantly. Reduce heat to medium.
Boil gently, uncovered, for about 25 minutes, stirring often, until mixture
gels when tested on small cold plate (see Tip, page 77).

Add remaining 3 ingredients. Stir. Fill 5 hot sterile 1 cup (250 mL) jars to
within 1/4 inch (6 mm) of top. Remove air bubbles and adjust headspace
if necessary. Wipe rims. Place hot metal lids on jars and screw on metal
bands fingertip tight. Do not over-tighten. Process in boiling water bath
for 20 minutes (see page 9). Remove jars. Let stand at room temperature
until cool. Makes about 5 3/4 cups (1.45 L).

1 tbsp. (15 mL): 60 Calories; 1 g Total Fat (0 g Mono, 0 g Poly, 0 g Sat); 0 mg Cholesterol;
12 g Carbohydrate; 0 g Fibre; 0 g Protein; 0 mg Sodium

Red Grape Preserves

Sweet red grapes combine with blueberries to create a delightful jewel-toned preserve. These sweet preserves are perfect for serving over pancakes, French toast or waffles, or for stirring into yogurt.

Granulated sugar	5 cups	1.25 L
Chopped seedless red grapes	3 cups	750 mL
Fresh (or frozen, thawed) blueberries	1 cup	250 mL
Water	1/4 cup	60 mL
Bottled lemon juice	1 tbsp.	15 mL
Pouch of liquid pectin	3 oz.	85 mL

Combine first 5 ingredients in Dutch oven. Bring to a hard boil, stirring constantly.

Add pectin. Boil hard for 1 minute, stirring constantly. Remove from heat. Skim and discard foam. Stir for 5 minutes to suspend solids. Fill 6 hot sterile 1 cup (250 mL) jars to within 1/4 inch (6 mm) of top. Remove air bubbles and adjust headspace if necessary. Wipe rims. Place hot metal lids on jars and screw on metal bands fingertip tight. Do not over-tighten. Process in boiling water bath for 15 minutes (see page 9). Remove jars. Let stand at room temperature until cool. Makes about 6 cups (1.5 L).

1 tbsp. (15 mL): 45 Calories; 0 g Total Fat (0 g Mono, 0 g Poly, 0 g Sat); 0 mg Cholesterol; 11 g Carbohydrate; 0 g Fibre; 0 g Protein; 0 mg Sodium

1. Smoky Pear Salsa, page 23
2. Eggplant Salsa, page 45

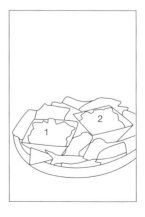

Ginger Pear Conserve

This conserve contains plenty of pears and a good dose of gingery bite.
Macadamia nuts add a bit of crunch to this soft spread that's simply divine
served on toast, bagels, cake or waffles.

Chopped peeled firm pear (see Tip, page 14)	6 cups	1.5 L
Granulated sugar	4 cups	1 L
Finely chopped crystallized ginger	3/4 cup	175 mL
Finely chopped ginger root	1/2 cup	125 mL
Lime juice	1/2 cup	125 mL
Water	1/2 cup	125 mL
Chopped salted, roasted macadamia nuts	1/2 cup	125 mL
Grated lime zest (see Tip, page 31)	1 tsp.	5 mL

Combine first 6 ingredients in Dutch oven. Bring to a boil, stirring often. Reduce heat to medium. Boil gently, uncovered, for about 40 minutes, stirring occasionally, until mixture is thickened and forms a soft gel when tested on small cold plate (see Tip, page 77). Remove from heat.

Add nuts and zest. Stir. Fill 6 hot sterile 1 cup (250 mL) jars to within 1/4 inch (6 mm) of top. Remove air bubbles and adjust headspace if necessary. Wipe rims. Place hot metal lids on jars and screw on metal bands fingertip tight. Do not over-tighten. Process in boiling water bath for 15 minutes (see page 9). Remove jars. Let stand at room temperature until cool. Makes about 6 cups (1.5 L).

1 tbsp. (15 mL): 50 Calories; 0.5 g Total Fat (0 g Mono, 0 g Poly, 0 g Sat); 0 mg Cholesterol; 11 g Carbohydrate; 0 g Fibre; 0 g Protein; 0 mg Sodium

1. Rhubarb Jam, page 70
2. Orange Marmalade, page 80

Chunky Applesauce

This recipe is perfect for those that like their applesauce with plenty of character. This aromatic blend of apples and cinnamon tastes almost like apple crisp filling.

Chopped peeled cooking apple, such as McIntosh (see Tip, page 14)	8 cups	2 L
Granulated sugar	3/4 cup	175 mL
Water	3/4 cup	175 mL
Bottled lemon juice	2 tbsp.	30 mL
Ground cinnamon	1/2 tsp.	2 mL
Ground allspice	1/4 tsp.	1 mL

Combine all 6 ingredients in Dutch oven. Bring to a boil, stirring occasionally. Reduce heat to medium. Cook, uncovered, for about 10 minutes, stirring occasionally, until apples are tender. Remove from heat. Transfer half of apple mixture to blender or food processor. Carefully process until smooth (see Safety Tip). Return to pot. Stir. Fill 4 hot sterile 1 cup (250 mL) jars to within 1/2 inch (12 mm) of top. Remove air bubbles and adjust headspace if necessary. Wipe rims. Place hot metal lids on jars and screw on metal bands fingertip tight. Do not over-tighten. Process in boiling water bath for 15 minutes (see page 9). Remove jars. Let stand at room temperature until cool. Makes about 4 1/2 cups (1.1 L).

2 tbsp. (30 mL): 30 Calories; 0 g Total Fat (0 g Mono, 0 g Poly, 0 g Sat); 0 mg Cholesterol; 7 g Carbohydrate; 0 g Fibre; 0 g Protein; 0 mg Sodium

Safety Tip: Follow manufacturer's instructions for processing hot liquids.

Pineapple Ginger Preserves

There's plenty of great ginger flavour in these sweet, syrupy pineapple preserves. A great topping for ice cream, cake or yogurt.

Chopped fresh pineapple	5 cups	1.25 L
(about 1/2 inch, 12 mm, pieces)		
Granulated sugar	3 3/4 cups	925 mL
Bottled lemon juice	1/4 cup	60 mL
Finely grated ginger root	1 tbsp.	15 mL

Combine first 3 ingredients in Dutch oven. Heat and stir on medium until sugar is dissolved and mixture comes to a hard boil. Boil hard for about 20 minutes, stirring often, until mixture is thickened and forms a soft gel when tested on small cold plate (see Tip, page 77).

Stir in ginger. Fill 7 hot sterile 1/2 cup (125 mL) jars to within 1/4 inch (6 mm) of top. Remove air bubbles and adjust headspace if necessary. Wipe rims. Place hot metal lids on jars and screw on metal bands fingertip tight. Do not over-tighten. Process in boiling water bath for 20 minutes (see page 9). Remove jars. Let stand at room temperature until cool. Makes about 4 cups (1 L).

1 tbsp. (15 mL): 50 Calories; 0 g Total Fat (0 g Mono, 0 g Poly, 0 g Sat); 0 mg Cholesterol; 13 g Carbohydrate; 0 g Fibre; 0 g Protein; 0 mg Sodium

Apple Pear Pie Filling

This sweet-tart pie filling is loaded with textured fruit and plump raisins. Use two jars to make a 9-inch (23 cm) pie.

Chopped peeled pear (see Tip, page 14)	6 cups	1.5 L
Apple juice	1/3 cup	75 mL
Brown sugar, packed	1 1/2 cups	375 mL
Bottled lemon juice	1/2 cup	125 mL
Ground cinnamon	1 tsp.	5 mL
Ground nutmeg	1/4 tsp.	1 mL
Sliced peeled tart apple, such as Granny Smith (see Tip, page 14)	8 cups	2 L
Chopped golden raisins	1 cup	250 mL

Combine pear and apple juice in Dutch oven. Bring to a boil. Reduce heat to medium. Cook, uncovered, for about 10 minutes, stirring occasionally, until pear is tender. Carefully process in batches in blender or food processor until smooth (see Safety Tip). Return to same pot.

Add next 4 ingredients. Stir. Bring to a boil on medium. Boil gently, uncovered, for about 45 minutes, stirring often, until thickened enough to mound on a spoon.

Add apple and raisins. Stir. Cook, uncovered, for about 10 minutes, stirring occasionally, until heated through. Fill 3 hot sterile 2 cup (500 mL) jars to within 1 inch (2.5 cm) of top. Remove air bubbles and adjust headspace if necessary. Wipe rims. Place hot metal lids on jars and screw on metal bands fingertip tight. Do not over-tighten. Process in boiling water bath for 20 minutes (see page 9). Remove jars. Let stand at room temperature until cool. Makes about 6 cups (1.5 L).

1/4 cup (60 mL): 120 Calories; 0 g Total Fat (0 g Mono, 0 g Poly, 0 g Sat); 0 mg Cholesterol; 31 g Carbohydrate; 2 g Fibre; 0 g Protein; 10 mg Sodium

Safety Tip: Follow manufacturer's instructions for processing hot liquids.

Rhubarb Cherry Filling

This mildly tart filling makes perfect rhubarb pies. Use two jars to make a
9 inch (23 cm) pie and mix in 2 tablespoons (30 mL) of instant tapioca.

Chopped fresh (or frozen) rhubarb	7 cups	1.75 L
Chopped peeled tart apple, such as	4 cups	1 L
Granny Smith (see Tip, page 14)		
Granulated sugar	2 cups	500 mL
Bottled lemon juice	1/4 cup	60 mL
Chopped sweet cherries	3 cups	750 mL

Combine first 4 ingredients in Dutch oven. Bring to a boil, stirring constantly. Reduce heat to medium. Cook, uncovered, for about 30 minutes, stirring often, until thickened.

Add cherries. Stir. Fill 3 hot sterile 2 cup (500 mL) jars to within 1 inch (2.5 cm) of top. Remove air bubbles and adjust headspace if necessary. Wipe rims. Place hot metal lids on jars and screw on metal bands fingertip tight. Do not over-tighten. Process in boiling water bath for 20 minutes (see page 9). Remove jars. Let stand at room temperature until cool. Makes about 6 1/3 cups (1.6 L).

1/4 cup (60 mL): 80 Calories; 0 g Total Fat (0 g Mono, 0 g Poly, 0 g Sat); 0 mg Cholesterol;
21 g Carbohydrate; 1 g Fibre; 0 g Protein; 0 mg Sodium

Fig Strawberry Conserve

A nice, thick spread that's very versatile. Strawberries add sweetness, and figs seeds add a little crunch. Enjoy it served on toast, with cheese or roasted meats.

Coarsely chopped fresh figs	3 cups	750 mL
Coarsely chopped fresh strawberries	3 cups	750 mL
Water	3 cups	750 mL
Chopped dried figs	1/2 cup	125 mL
Bottled lemon juice	1/3 cup	75 mL
Ground cinnamon	1/2 tsp.	2 mL
Granulated sugar	4 cups	1 L
Finely chopped walnuts, toasted (see Tip, page 50)	1/4 cup	60 mL

Combine first 6 ingredients in Dutch oven. Bring to a boil on medium. Boil gently, uncovered, for 20 minutes, stirring occasionally.

Add sugar. Bring to a hard boil, stirring constantly. Boil hard for about 30 minutes, stirring often, until mixture gels when tested on small cold plate (see Tip, page 77). Remove from heat.

Stir in walnuts. Fill 5 hot sterile 1 cup (250 mL) jars to within 1/4 inch (6 mm) of top. Remove air bubbles and adjust headspace if necessary. Wipe rims. Place hot metal lids on jars and screw on metal bands fingertip-tight. Do not over-tighten. Process in boiling water bath for 15 minutes (see page 9). Remove jars. Let stand at room temperature until cool. Makes about 5 1/4 cups (1.3 L).

1 tbsp. (15 mL): 45 Calories; 0 g Total Fat (0 g Mono, 0 g Poly, 0 g Sat); 0 mg Cholesterol; 12 g Carbohydrate; 0 g Fibre; 0 g Protein; 0 mg Sodium

Spiced Wine Pears

Store-bought canned pears are decidedly boring in comparison to this deliciously spiced version. Wine makes these pears absolutely elegant. Any leftover syrup can be served over ice cream, pancakes or waffles.

Dry white wine	4 cups	1 L
Granulated sugar	2 cups	500 mL
Ground cardamom	1 tsp.	5 mL
Ground cinnamon	1 tsp.	5 mL
Ground allspice	1/4 tsp.	1 mL
Quartered firm ripe peeled pear (see Tip, page 14), about 10 pears	10 cups	2.5 L

Combine first 5 ingredients in Dutch oven. Bring to a boil, stirring occasionally.

Add pear. Stir. Reduce heat to medium. Cook, uncovered, for 5 minutes, stirring occasionally. Remove from heat. Using slotted spoon, fill 5 hot sterile 2 cup (500 mL) jars with pears to within 1 inch (2.5 cm) of top. Add hot wine mixture to jars to within 1/2 inch (12 mm) of top. Remove air bubbles and adjust headspace if necessary. Wipe rims. Place hot metal lids on jars and screw on metal bands fingertip tight. Do not over-tighten. Process in boiling water bath for 25 minutes (see page 9). Turn off heat. Let stand, uncovered, for 5 minutes. Remove jars. Let stand at room temperature until cool. Makes about 10 cups (2.5 L).

1/4 cup (60 mL): 80 Calories; 0 g Total Fat (0 g Mono, 0 g Poly, 0 g Sat); 0 mg Cholesterol; 17 g Carbohydrate; 1 g Fibre; 0 g Protein; 0 mg Sodium

Brandied Cran-Cherries

Serve this easy-to-make preserve over cake or ice cream, or mixed with sparkling wine. It also makes a great gift!

Water	2 cups	500 mL
Granulated sugar	1 1/2 cups	375 mL
Lemon juice	1/4 cup	60 mL
Pitted sweet cherries	4 cups	1 L
Fresh (or frozen, thawed) cranberries	3 cups	750 mL
Brandy	1 cup	250 mL

Combine first 3 ingredients in large saucepan. Bring to a boil, stirring occasionally.

Fill 8 hot sterile 1 cup (250 mL) jars with cherries and cranberries to within 1 inch (2.5 cm) of top. Add 2 tbsp. (30 mL) brandy to each jar. Add hot syrup mixture to within 1/2 inch (12 mm) of top. Remove air bubbles and adjust headspace if necessary. Wipe rims. Place hot metal lids on jars and screw on metal bands fingertip tight. Do not over-tighten. Process in boiling water bath for 15 minutes (see page 9). Turn off heat. Let stand, uncovered, for 5 minutes. Remove jars. Let stand at room temperature until cool. Makes about 8 cups (2 L).

2 tbsp. (30 mL): 30 Calories; 0 g Total Fat (0 g Mono, 0 g Poly, 0 g Sat); 0 mg Cholesterol; 6 g Carbohydrate; 0 g Fibre; 0 g Protein; 0 mg Sodium

Citrus Apricot Marmalade

This thick, spreadable citrus marmalade has lovely notes of sweet and tangy apricot for a unique twist on this traditional favourite.

Medium lemons (see Tip, page 65)	2	2
Medium orange (see Tip, page 65)	1	1
Water	3 cups	750 mL
Lemon juice	1/2 cup	125 mL
Box of pectin crystals	2 oz.	57 g
Granulated sugar	5 cups	1.25 L
Thinly sliced dried apricot	2 cups	500 mL

Remove rind from lemons and orange using vegetable peeler. Cut rind into 1/8 x 1 inch (0.3 x 2.5 cm) strips. Transfer to Dutch oven. Line medium bowl with 16 inch (40 cm) square of double-layered cheesecloth. Cut lemons and oranges into quarters. Squeeze juice into cheesecloth-lined bowl. Place squeezed fruit pieces in centre of cheesecloth square. Draw up corners and tie with butcher's string. Add cheesecloth bag and juice to Dutch oven.

Add water and lemon juice. Stir. Bring to a boil. Reduce heat to medium. Boil gently, uncovered, for about 30 minutes, stirring occasionally, until rind is softened. Remove and discard cheesecloth bag.

Add pectin. Bring to a boil, stirring constantly.

Add sugar and apricot. Bring to a hard boil, stirring constantly. Boil hard for 1 minute, stirring constantly. Remove from heat. Stir for 5 minutes to suspend solids. Fill 5 hot sterile 1 cup (250 mL) jars to within 1/4 inch (6 mm) of top. Remove air bubbles and adjust headspace if necessary. Wipe rims. Place hot metal lids on jars and screw on metal bands fingertip tight. Do not over-tighten. Process in boiling water bath for 15 minutes (see page 9). Remove jars. Let stand at room temperature until cool. Makes about 5 2/3 cups (1.4 L).

1 tbsp. (15 mL): 45 Calories; 0 g Total Fat (0 g Mono, 0 g Poly, 0 g Sat); 0 mg Cholesterol; 12 g Carbohydrate; 0 g Fibre; 0 g Protein; 0 mg Sodium

Zucchini Pepper Marmalade

This is certainly not your run-of-the-mill marmalade. Zucchini, red pepper and crushed chilies give this sweet and lemony mixture plenty of character. Use this marmalade the same as you'd use jalapeño jelly.

Large lemons (see Tip, page 65)	2	2
Bottled lemon juice	1/3 cup	75 mL
Water	1/4 cup	60 mL
Grated zucchini (with peel)	3 cups	750 mL
Finely chopped red pepper	1 cup	250 mL
Box of pectin crystals	2 oz.	57 g
Dried crushed chilies	1 tsp.	5 mL
Granulated sugar	5 cups	1.25 L

Remove rind from lemons using vegetable peeler. Finely chop rind. Transfer to Dutch oven. Remove and discard pith from lemons. Segment lemons over pot to catch juices (see Tip, page 146). Finely chop segments. Add to pot.

Add lemon juice and water. Bring to a boil. Reduce heat to medium-low. Simmer, covered, for about 10 minutes until rind is softened.

Add next 4 ingredients. Bring to a boil, stirring constantly.

Add sugar. Bring to a hard boil, stirring constantly. Boil hard for 1 minute, stirring constantly. Remove from heat. Stir for 5 minutes to suspend solids. Fill 5 hot sterile 1 cup (250 mL) jars to within 1/4 inch (6 mm) of top. Remove air bubbles and adjust headspace if necessary. Wipe rims. Place hot metal lids on jars and screw on metal bands fingertip tight. Do not over-tighten. Process in boiling water bath for 15 minutes (see page 9). Remove jars. Let stand at room temperature until cool. Makes about 5 3/4 cups (1.45 L).

1 tbsp. (15 mL): 45 Calories; 0 g Total Fat (0 g Mono, 0 g Poly, 0 g Sat); 0 mg Cholesterol; 11 g Carbohydrate; 0 g Fibre; 0 g Protein; 0 mg Sodium

Peach Salsa Jam

If you just love salsa flavours, why not combine them with the classic peach jam? This fabulous concoction pairs peach sweetness with tomato, onion and spicy chili paste for an absolutely unique glaze for pork, ham or chicken.

Finely chopped peeled peach (see Tip, page 129)	2 1/2 cups	625 mL
Chopped seeded Roma (plum) tomato	1 cup	250 mL
Finely chopped onion	1/2 cup	125 mL
Bottled lemon juice	1/3 cup	75 mL
Box of pectin crystals	2 oz.	57 g
Chili paste (sambal oelek)	1 tsp.	5 mL
Granulated sugar	6 cups	1.5 L

Stir first 6 ingredients in Dutch oven until pectin is dissolved. Bring to a boil, stirring often.

Add sugar. Bring to a hard boil, stirring constantly. Boil hard for 1 minute, stirring constantly. Remove from heat. Stir for 5 minutes to suspend solids. Fill 6 hot sterile 1 cup (250 mL) jars to within 1/4 inch (6 mm) of top. Remove air bubbles and adjust headspace if necessary. Wipe rims. Place hot metal lids on jars and screw on metal bands fingertip tight. Do not over-tighten. Process in boiling water bath for 15 minutes (see page 9). Remove jars. Let stand at room temperature until cool. Makes about 6 cups (1.5 L).

1 tbsp. (15 mL): 50 Calories; 0 g Total Fat (0 g Mono, 0 g Poly, 0 g Sat); 0 mg Cholesterol; 14 g Carbohydrate; 0 g Fibre; 0 g Protein; 0 mg Sodium

 tip To thoroughly clean fresh fruit for preserving, scrub with a vegetable brush under hot water to remove any pesticides or wax residue.

Pear and Strawberry Jam

No one will ever suggest that this jam is dull. Its bold orangey-red colour makes it memorable—and it's got the lovely flavours of sweet pears and strawberries to boot!

Finely chopped peeled pear (see Tip, page 14)	3 cups	750 mL
Crushed fresh strawberries	1 1/2 cups	375 mL
Box of pectin crystals	2 oz.	57 g
White wine vinegar	2 tbsp.	30 mL
Bottled lemon juice	1 tbsp.	15 mL
Granulated sugar	5 cups	1.25 L

Stir first 5 ingredients in Dutch oven until pectin is dissolved. Bring to a boil, stirring constantly.

Add sugar. Bring to a hard boil, stirring constantly. Boil hard for 1 minute, stirring constantly. Remove from heat. Skim and discard foam. Stir for 5 minutes to suspend solids. Fill 6 hot sterile 1 cup (250 mL) jars to within 1/4 inch (6 mm) of top. Remove air bubbles and adjust headspace if necessary. Wipe rims. Place hot metal lids on jars and screw on metal bands fingertip tight. Do not over-tighten. Process in boiling water bath for 15 minutes (see page 9). Remove jars. If jam does not set the following day, let stand in a cool, dark place for 1 to 2 weeks until set. Makes about 6 cups (1.5 L).

1 tbsp. (15 mL): 45 Calories; 0 g Total Fat (0 g Mono, 0 g Poly, 0 g Sat); 0 mg Cholesterol; 11 g Carbohydrate; 0 g Fibre; 0 g Protein; 0 mg Sodium

Cinnamon Crabapple Jelly

This attractive, pale-pink jelly has a pure, sweet apple flavour with distinctive cinnamon lingering in the background. This nostalgic-tasting jelly has a certain old-fashioned charm to it!

Crabapples, stems and blossoms removed, quartered	6 lbs.	2.7 kg
Water	6 cups	1.5 L
Cinnamon sticks (4 inches, 10 cm, each)	3	3
Piece of ginger root (1 inch, 2.5 cm, length), chopped	1	1
Whole cloves	1 tsp.	5 mL
Box of pectin crystals	2 oz.	57 g
Bottled lemon juice	2 tbsp.	30 mL
Granulated sugar	7 cups	1.75 L

Combine first 5 ingredients in large pot. Bring to a boil, stirring occasionally. Reduce heat to medium-low. Simmer, uncovered, for about 30 minutes, crushing occasionally with potato masher, until softened. Carefully strain through sieve or colander lined with double layer of damp cheesecloth into large bowl. Let stand for 3 hours. Do not squeeze solids. Discard solids. Measure 5 cups (1.25 L) juice into Dutch oven.

Add pectin and lemon juice. Stir until pectin is dissolved. Bring to a boil, stirring constantly.

Add sugar. Bring to a hard boil, stirring constantly. Boil hard for 1 minute, stirring constantly. Remove from heat. Skim and discard foam. Fill 8 hot sterile 1 cup (250 mL) jars to within 1/4 inch (6 mm) of top. Remove air bubbles and adjust headspace if necessary. Wipe rims. Place hot metal lids on jars and screw on metal bands fingertip tight. Do not over-tighten. Process in boiling water bath for 15 minutes (see page 9). Remove jars. Let stand at room temperature until cool. Makes about 8 1/2 cups (2.1 L).

1 tbsp. (15 mL): 50 Calories; 0 g Total Fat (0 g Mono, 0 g Poly, 0 g Sat); 0 mg Cholesterol; 14 g Carbohydrate; trace Fibre; 0 g Protein; 0 mg Sodium

Lemon Peach Marmalade

Bright, fresh flavours abound in this cheery freezer marmalade. Your microwave makes quick work of softening the rind, and an easy freezer method saves you plenty of time and effort!

Finely chopped peeled peach (see Tip, page 129)	3 1/2 cups	875 mL
Lemon juice	1 tbsp.	15 mL
Medium lemons (see Tip, page 65)	2	2
Water	1 tbsp.	15 mL
Granulated sugar	1 1/2 cups	375 mL
Envelope of freezer jam pectin	1.59 oz.	45 g

Stir peach and lemon juice in large bowl.

Remove rind from lemons using vegetable peeler. Finely chop rind. Transfer to small microwave-safe bowl. Add water. Microwave, covered, on high (100%) for about 2 minutes until softened (see Note). Add to peach mixture. Remove and discard pith from lemons. Segment lemons over separate large bowl to catch juices (see Tip, page 146). Finely chop segments. Add segments and juice to peach mixture.

Stir sugar and pectin in small bowl until combined. Add to peach mixture. Stir for 3 minutes. Fill clean plastic containers to within 1/2 inch (12 mm) of top (see Tip, page 79). Wipe rims. Let stand at room temperature for about 30 minutes until thickened. Cover with tight fitting lids. Store in refrigerator for up to 3 weeks or in freezer for up to 1 year. Makes about 4 1/4 cups (1 L).

1 tbsp. (15 mL): 25 Calories; 0 g Total Fat (0 g Mono, 0 g Poly, 0 g Sat); 0 mg Cholesterol; 7 g Carbohydrate; 0 g Fibre; 0 g Protein; 0 mg Sodium

Note: The microwaves used in our test kitchen are 900 watts—but microwaves are sold in many different powers. You should be able to find the wattage of yours by opening the door and looking for the mandatory label. If your microwave is more than 900 watts, you may need to reduce the cooking time. If it's less than 900 watts, you'll probably need to increase the cooking time.

Shiraz Plum Jam

Bits of plum are perfectly suspended in this colourful jam boasting lovely notes of shiraz. This jam makes a great addition to a holiday gift basket, and is absolutely decadent when served with sharp cheeses.

Finely chopped black (or red) plums (about 2 1/2 lbs., 1.1 kg)	7 cups	1.75 L
Shiraz (or cabernet) red wine	1/2 cup	125 mL
Chinese five-spice powder	1/2 tsp.	2 mL
Box of pectin crystals	2 oz.	57 g
Granulated sugar	7 cups	1.75 L

Stir first 4 ingredients in large pot until pectin is dissolved. Bring to a boil, stirring constantly.

Add sugar. Bring to a hard boil, stirring constantly. Boil hard for 1 minute, stirring constantly. Remove from heat. Stir for 5 minutes to suspend solids. Fill 8 hot sterile 1 cup (250 mL) jars to within 1/4 inch (6 mm) of top. Remove air bubbles and adjust headspace if necessary. Wipe rims. Place hot metal lids on jars and screw on metal bands fingertip tight. Do not over-tighten. Process in boiling water bath for 15 minutes (see page 9). Remove jars. Let stand at room temperature until cool. Makes about 8 1/2 cups (2.1 L).

1 tbsp. (15 mL): 45 Calories; 0 g Total Fat (0 g Mono, 0 g Poly, 0 g Sat); 0 mg Cholesterol; 11 g Carbohydrate; 0 g Fibre; 0 g Protein; 0 mg Sodium

Rhubarb Jam

Rhubarb flavour really shines in this jewel-toned jam that's just perfect. Cranberries add a little sweetness to this rather tart combination for a nicely balanced spread that's great on toast or bagels.

Finely chopped fresh (or frozen) rhubarb	5 cups	1.25 L
Chopped dried cranberries	1 cup	250 mL
Cranberry cocktail	1 cup	250 mL
Box of pectin crystals	2 oz.	57 g
Granulated sugar	6 cups	1.5 L

Stir first 4 ingredients in Dutch oven until pectin is dissolved. Bring to a boil, stirring constantly.

Add sugar. Bring to a hard boil, stirring constantly. Boil hard for 1 minute, stirring constantly. Remove from heat. Stir for 5 minutes to suspend solids. Fill 6 hot sterile 1 cup (250 mL) jars to within 1/4 inch (6 mm) of top. Remove air bubbles and adjust headspace if necessary. Wipe rims. Place hot metal lids on jars and screw on metal bands fingertip tight. Do not over-tighten. Process in boiling water bath for 15 minutes (see page 9). Remove jars. Let stand at room temperature until cool. Makes 6 1/3 cups (1.6 L).

1 tbsp. (15 mL): 50 Calories; 0 g Total Fat (0 g Mono, 0 g Poly, 0 g Sat); 0 mg Cholesterol; 13 g Carbohydrate; 0 g Fibre; 0 g Protein; 0 mg Sodium

Pictured on page 54.

1. Razz-Berry Syrup, page 129

Pomegranate Blueberry Jelly

Using pomegranate juice certainly eliminates the fuss of peeling pomegranates and extracting their juice. This quick recipe lets you make up a glistening jelly any time of year with minimal effort.

Blueberry pomegranate juice	3 1/2 cups	875 mL
Box of pectin crystals	2 oz.	57 g
Granulated sugar	5 cups	1.25 L

Stir juice and pectin in Dutch oven until pectin is dissolved. Bring to a boil, stirring constantly.

Add sugar. Bring to a hard boil, stirring constantly. Boil hard for 1 minute, stirring constantly. Fill 6 hot sterile 1 cup (250 mL) jars to within 1/4 inch (6 mm) of top. Remove air bubbles and adjust headspace if necessary. Wipe rims. Place hot metal lids on jars and screw on metal bands fingertip tight. Do not over-tighten. Process in boiling water bath for 15 minutes (see page 9). Remove jars. Let stand at room temperature until cool. Makes about 6 cups (1.5 L).

1 tbsp. (15 mL): 45 Calories; 0 g Total Fat (0 g Mono, 0 g Poly, 0 g Sat); 0 mg Cholesterol; 12 g Carbohydrate; 0 g Fibre; 0 g Protein; 0 mg Sodium

1. Lemon Garden Pickle Mix, page 119

Favourite Cherry Jam

This didn't become our favourite cherry jam without good reason.
It's so versatile that you can use it in Black Forest cake, sandwich cookies
or even in jam sandwiches! A hint of orange and cinnamon make this jam
truly memorable.

Granulated sugar	6 cups	1.5 L
Chopped sweet cherries	4 cups	1 L
Orange juice	1/3 cup	75 mL
Bottled lemon juice	2 tbsp.	30 mL
Grated orange zest (see Tip, page 31)	2 tsp.	10 mL
Cinnamon stick (4 inches, 10 cm)	1	1
Vanilla bean, split	1/2	1/2
Pouches of liquid pectin (3 oz., 85 mL, each)	2	2

Combine first 7 ingredients in Dutch oven. Bring to a hard boil, stirring constantly.

Add pectin. Boil hard for 1 minute, stirring constantly. Remove from heat. Skim and discard foam. Remove and discard cinnamon stick and vanilla bean. Stir for 5 minutes to suspend solids. Fill 6 hot sterile 1 cup (250 mL) jars to within 1/4 inch (6 mm) of top. Remove air bubbles and adjust headspace if necessary. Wipe rims. Place hot metal lids on jars and screw on metal bands fingertip tight. Do not over-tighten. Process in boiling water bath for 15 minutes (see page 9). Remove jars. Let stand at room temperature until cool. Makes about 6 1/2 cups (1.6 L).

1 tbsp. (15 mL): 45 Calories; 0 g Total Fat (0 g Mono, 0 g Poly, 0 g Sat); 0 mg Cholesterol;
12 g Carbohydrate; 0 g Fibre; 0 g Protein; 0 mg Sodium

Peach Blueberry Jam

Summer's favourite flavours combine in this colourful jam. This sweet
spread is made even better with the additions of lime and vanilla.

Finely chopped peeled peach (see Tip, page 129)	3 cups	750 mL
Crushed fresh (or frozen, thawed) blueberries	1 1/4 cups	300 mL
Lime juice	3 tbsp.	45 mL
Box of pectin crystals	2 oz.	57 g
Grated lime zest (see Tip, page 31)	1 tsp.	5 mL
Vanilla bean, split	1/2	1/2
Granulated sugar	5 cups	1.25 L

Stir first 6 ingredients in Dutch oven until pectin is dissolved. Bring to a boil, stirring constantly.

Add sugar. Bring to a hard boil, stirring constantly. Boil hard for 1 minute, stirring constantly. Remove from heat. Remove and discard vanilla bean. Skim and discard foam. Fill 6 hot sterile 1 cup (250 mL) jars to within 1/4 inch (6 mm) of top. Remove air bubbles and adjust headspace if necessary. Wipe rims. Place hot metal lids on jars and screw on metal bands fingertip tight. Do not over-tighten. Process in boiling water bath for 15 minutes (see page 9). Remove jars. Let stand at room temperature until cool. Makes about 6 cups (1.5 L).

1 tbsp. (15 mL): 45 Calories; 0 g Total Fat (0 g Mono, 0 g Poly, 0 g Sat); 0 mg Cholesterol; 12 g Carbohydrate; 0 g Fibre; 0 g Protein; 0 mg Sodium

Nectarine Jam

Capture the unadulterated flavour of fresh nectarines in a lovely jewel-toned jam. Bright flavours with lovely texture.

Chopped unpeeled nectarine	6 cups	1.5 L
Bottled lemon juice	1/4 cup	60 mL
Water	1/4 cup	60 mL
Box of pectin crystals	2 oz.	57 g
Granulated sugar	4 cups	1 L

Combine first 3 ingredients in Dutch oven. Bring to a boil on medium. Boil gently, uncovered, for about 10 minutes, stirring occasionally, until nectarine is softened.

Add pectin. Bring to a boil, stirring constantly.

Add sugar. Bring to a hard boil, stirring constantly. Boil hard for 1 minute, stirring constantly. Remove from heat. Skim and discard foam. Stir for 5 minutes to suspend solids. Fill 6 hot sterile 1 cup (250 mL) jars to within 1/4 inch (6 mm) of top. Remove air bubbles and adjust headspace if necessary. Wipe rims. Place hot metal lids on jars and screw on metal bands fingertip tight. Do not over-tighten. Process in boiling water bath for 15 minutes (see page 9). Remove jars. Let stand at room temperature until cool. Makes about 6 1/4 cups (1.5 L).

1 tbsp. (15 mL): 35 Calories; 0 g Total Fat (0 g Mono, 0 g Poly, 0 g Sat); 0 mg Cholesterol; 9 g Carbohydrate; 0 g Fibre; 0 g Protein; 0 mg Sodium

Pictured on page 90.

Strawberry Mango Freezer Jam

This lovely jam is so easy to make since no cooking is required! Enjoy fresh-picked strawberry flavour with a tropical twist from mango.

Granulated sugar	1 1/2 cups	375 mL
Envelope of freezer jam pectin	1.59 oz.	45 g
Crushed fresh strawberries	3 cups	750 mL
Finely chopped ripe mango	1 cup	250 mL
Lime juice	1 tbsp.	15 mL
Grated lime zest (see Tip, page 31)	1/2 tsp.	2 mL

Stir sugar and pectin in large bowl until combined.

Add remaining 4 ingredients. Stir for 3 minutes. Fill clean plastic containers to within 1/2 inch (12 mm) of top (see Tip, page 79). Wipe rims. Let stand at room temperature for about 30 minutes until thickened. Cover with tight-fitting lids. Store in refrigerator for up to 3 weeks or in freezer for up to 1 year. Makes about 5 cups (1.25 L).

1 tbsp. (15 mL): 15 Calories; 0 g Total Fat (0 g Mono, 0 g Poly, 0 g Sat); 0 mg Cholesterol; 4 g Carbohydrate; 0 g Fibre; 0 g Protein; 0 mg Sodium

Pictured on page 89.

 tip To make sure your preserves have reached the gelling point, remove them from heat, place a spoonful on a chilled plate and place it in the freezer until the mixture has reached room temperature. Press your finger down the middle of the mixture. If it doesn't run together into the groove you've created, the mixture has gelled. To prevent overcooking, don't leave your preserves simmering on the stove while you're testing.

Spicy Tequila Lime Jelly

Enjoy the flavours of sweet lime and tasty tequila in this savoury jelly. The jalapeño heat really builds, so be prepared for some serious kick! Serve with cheese and tortilla chips, or on roast pork or chicken.

Granulated sugar	3 cups	750 mL
Lime juice	1/3 cup	75 mL
Finely chopped fresh jalapeño pepper (see Tip, page 116)	1/4 cup	60 mL
Finely chopped red pepper	1/4 cup	60 mL
Finely chopped yellow pepper	1/4 cup	60 mL
White wine vinegar	1/4 cup	60 mL
Dried crushed chilies	1 tsp.	5 mL
Pouch of liquid pectin	3 oz.	85 mL
Tequila	1/4 cup	60 mL
Grated lime zest (see Tip, page 31)	1 tsp.	5 mL

Combine first 7 ingredients in Dutch oven. Bring to a hard boil, stirring constantly.

Add remaining 3 ingredients. Boil hard for 1 minute, stirring constantly. Remove from heat. Stir for 5 minutes to suspend solids. Fill 5 hot sterile 1/2 cup (125 mL) jars to within 1/4 inch (6 mm) of top. Remove air bubbles and adjust headspace if necessary. Wipe rims. Place hot metal lids on jars and screw on metal bands fingertip tight. Do not over-tighten. Process in boiling water bath for 15 minutes (see page 9). Remove jars. Let stand at room temperature until cool. Makes about 2 3/4 cups (675 mL).

2 tsp. (10 mL): 35 Calories; 0 g Total Fat (0 g Mono, 0 g Poly, 0 g Sat); 0 mg Cholesterol; 9 g Carbohydrate; 0 g Fibre; 0 g Protein; 0 mg Sodium

Pictured on page 143.

Apricot Pineapple Freezer Jam

This vibrant, golden, not-too-sweet jam packs toothsome bits of apricot and pineapple. Serve on toast, pancakes or warm buttered biscuits.

Granulated sugar	1 1/2 cups	375 mL
Envelope of freezer jam pectin	1.59 oz.	45 g
Finely chopped peeled apricot (see Tip, page 129)	4 cups	1 L
Can of crushed pineapple (with juice)	14 oz.	398 mL

Stir sugar and pectin in large bowl until combined.

Combine apricot and pineapple with juice in large saucepan. Bring to a boil. Reduce heat to medium. Cook, uncovered, for about 15 minutes, stirring occasionally, until apricot is softened. Add to pectin mixture. Stir for 3 minutes. Fill clean plastic containers to within 1/2 inch (12 mm) of top (see Tip, below). Wipe rims. Let stand at room temperature for about 1 hour until cool and thickened. Cover with tight-fitting lids. Store in refrigerator for up to 3 weeks or in freezer for up to 1 year. Makes about 5 cups (1.25 L).

1 tbsp. (15 mL): 20 Calories; 0 g Total Fat (0 g Mono, 0 g Poly, 0 g Sat); 0 mg Cholesterol; 5 g Carbohydrate; 0 g Fibre; 0 g Protein; 0 mg Sodium

 tip When using plastic containers for freezing preserves, select containers without any cracks or leaks. Plastic freezing jars designed to store preserves in the freezer are also available at many grocery stores. See also page 8.

Orange Marmalade

This cheery marmalade follows tradition perfectly. Bright citrusy flavours, not too sweet and not too bitter. A wonderful balance of orange and lemon.

Medium oranges (see Tip, page 65)	6	6
Small lemons (see Tip, page 65)	3	3
Water	1 cup	250 mL
Box of pectin crystals	2 oz.	57 g
Granulated sugar	6 cups	1.5 L

Remove rind from oranges and lemons using vegetable peeler. Finely chop rind from 4 oranges and 2 lemons. Transfer to Dutch oven. Discard remaining rind. Remove and discard pith from fruit. Segment fruit over pot to catch juices (see Tip, page 146). Finely chop segments. Add to pot.

Add water. Bring to a boil. Reduce heat to medium-low. Simmer, covered, for 15 minutes.

Add pectin. Bring to a boil, stirring constantly.

Add sugar. Bring to a hard boil, stirring constantly. Boil hard for 1 minute, stirring constantly. Remove from heat. Stir for 5 minutes to suspend solids. Fill 6 hot sterile 1 cup (250 mL) jars to within 1/4 inch (6 mm) of top. Remove air bubbles and adjust headspace if necessary. Wipe rims. Place hot metal lids on jars and screw on metal bands fingertip tight. Do not over-tighten. Process in boiling water bath for 15 minutes (see page 9). Remove jars. Let stand at room temperature until cool. Makes about 7 cups (1.75 L).

1 tbsp. (15 mL): 45 Calories; 0 g Total Fat (0 g Mono, 0 g Poly, 0 g Sat); 0 mg Cholesterol; 12 g Carbohydrate; 0 g Fibre; 0 g Protein; 0 mg Sodium

Pictured on page 54.

Raspberry Jam

This fragrant, cheerful spread contains little raspberry seeds to add that perfect amount of crunch. A little sweet, and not too tart. Delightful served on toast or in peanut butter and jam sandwiches.

Crushed fresh (or frozen, thawed) raspberries (about 2 1/2 lbs., 1.1 kg)	5 cups	1.25 L
Box of pectin crystals	2 oz.	57 g
Bottled lemon juice	2 tbsp.	30 mL
Granulated sugar	7 cups	1.75 L

Stir first 3 ingredients in Dutch oven until pectin is dissolved. Bring to a boil, stirring constantly.

Add sugar. Bring to a hard boil, stirring constantly. Boil hard for 1 minute, stirring constantly. Remove from heat. Skim and discard foam. Fill 8 hot sterile 1 cup (250 mL) jars to within 1/4 inch (6 mm) of top. Remove air bubbles and adjust headspace if necessary. Wipe rims. Place hot metal lids on jars and screw on metal bands fingertip tight. Do not over-tighten. Process in boiling water bath for 15 minutes (see page 9). Remove jars. Let stand at room temperature until cool. Makes about 8 cups (2 L).

1 tbsp. (15 mL): 45 Calories; 0 g Total Fat (0 g Mono, 0 g Poly, 0 g Sat); 0 mg Cholesterol; 11 g Carbohydrate; 0 g Fibre; 0 g Protein; 0 mg Sodium

Curry Mango Jelly

Use any variety of mango juice blend to make this sweet-and-savoury jelly.
Good with cheese and crackers or as a glaze on pork and chicken.

Mango orange juice	3 1/2 cups	875 mL
White wine vinegar	1/2 cup	125 mL
Finely chopped ripe (or frozen, thawed) mango	1 cup	250 mL
Box of pectin crystals	2 oz.	57 g
Hot curry powder	1 tbsp.	15 mL
Granulated sugar	5 cups	1.25 L

Stir first 5 ingredients in Dutch oven until pectin is dissolved. Bring to a boil, stirring constantly.

Add sugar. Bring to a hard boil, stirring constantly. Boil hard for 1 minute, stirring constantly. Remove from heat. Skim and discard foam. Stir for 5 minutes to suspend solids. Fill 6 hot sterile 1 cup (250 mL) jars to within 1/4 inch (6 mm) of top. Remove air bubbles and adjust headspace if necessary. Wipe rims. Place hot metal lids on jars and screw on metal bands fingertip tight. Do not over-tighten. Process in boiling water bath for 15 minutes (see page 9). Remove jars. Let stand at room temperature until cool. Makes about 6 1/2 cups (1.6 L).

1 tbsp. (15 mL): 45 Calories; 0 g Total Fat (0 g Mono, 0 g Poly, 0 g Sat); 0 mg Cholesterol; 11 g Carbohydrate; 0 g Fibre; 0 g Protein; 0 mg Sodium

Pictured on page 126.

Double Pepper Strawberry Jam

This lovely strawberry jam has a subtle heat that builds. Black pepper and crushed chilies make this jam both unique and very tasty!

Crushed fresh strawberries (about 2 1/2 lbs., 1.1 kg)	5 cups	1.25 L
Box of pectin crystals	2 oz.	57 g
Balsamic vinegar	3 tbsp.	45 mL
Bottled lemon juice	2 tbsp.	30 mL
Granulated sugar	6 cups	1.5 L
Coarsely ground pepper	1/2 tsp.	2 mL
Dried crushed chilies	1/2 tsp.	2 mL

Stir first 4 ingredients in large pot until pectin is dissolved. Bring to a boil, stirring constantly.

Add sugar. Bring to a hard boil, stirring constantly. Boil hard for 1 minute, stirring constantly.

Stir in pepper and chilies. Remove from heat. Skim and discard foam. Stir for 5 minutes to suspend solids. Fill 7 hot sterile 1 cup (250 mL) jars to within 1/4 inch (6 mm) of top. Remove air bubbles and adjust headspace if necessary. Wipe rims. Place hot metal lids on jars and screw on metal bands fingertip tight. Do not over-tighten. Process in boiling water bath for 15 minutes (see page 9). Remove jars. Let stand at room temperature until cool. Makes about 7 cups (1.75 mL).

1 tbsp. (15 mL): 45 Calories; 0 g Total Fat (0 g Mono, 0 g Poly, 0 g Sat); 0 mg Cholesterol; 11 g Carbohydrate; 0 g Fibre; 0 g Protein; 0 mg Sodium

Cranberry Port Jelly

This burgundy-coloured jelly is just a little bit sweet with a mild tanginess from apricot—plus you're sure to enjoy the decidedly elegant flavour of port. This jelly goes great with cheese or roast meats, or on toast.

Fresh (or frozen) cranberries	3 cups	750 mL
Water	2 1/2 cups	625 mL
Chopped unpeeled tart apple (such as Granny Smith)	1 cup	250 mL
Piece of ginger root (1 inch, 2.5 cm, length), sliced	1	1
Cinnamon stick (4 inches, 10 cm)	1	1
Whole black peppercorns	1 tsp.	5 mL
Port wine	2 cups	500 mL
Box of pectin crystals	2 oz.	57 g
Bottled lemon juice	2 tbsp.	30 mL
Granulated sugar	3 1/2 cups	875 mL

Combine first 6 ingredients in Dutch oven. Bring to a boil, stirring occasionally. Reduce heat to medium-low. Simmer, covered, for about 30 minutes, crushing occasionally with potato masher, until fruit is softened. Remove from heat. Carefully strain through colander lined with double layer of damp cheesecloth into large bowl. Let stand for 1 hour. Do not squeeze solids. Discard solids. Measure 1 1/2 cups (375 mL) liquid into Dutch oven.

Add next 3 ingredients. Stir until pectin is dissolved. Bring to a boil, stirring constantly.

Add sugar. Bring to a hard boil, stirring constantly. Boil hard for 2 minutes, stirring constantly. Remove from heat. Fill 4 hot sterile 1 cup (250 mL) jars to within 1/4 inch (6 mm) of top. Remove air bubbles and adjust headspace if necessary. Wipe rims. Place hot metal lids on jars and screw on metal bands fingertip tight. Do not over-tighten. Process in boiling water bath for 15 minutes (see page 9). Remove jars. Let stand at room temperature until cool. Makes about 4 3/4 cups (1.2 L).

1 tbsp. (15 mL): 50 Calories; 0 g Total Fat (0 g Mono, 0 g Poly, 0 g Sat); 0 mg Cholesterol; 11 g Carbohydrate; 0 g Fibre; 0 g Protein; 0 mg Sodium

Onion Garlic Jam

If you just can't get enough onion and garlic, this jam is for you. This darkly coloured jam packs plenty of flavour, with distinctive notes of wine lingering in the background. Try it with a sharp cheese or goat cheese.

Thinly sliced onion (quartered and sliced crosswise)	2 cups	500 mL
Thinly sliced garlic cloves	1/2 cup	125 mL
Brown sugar, packed	1/4 cup	60 mL
White vinegar	1/4 cup	60 mL
Dry white wine	2 1/2 cups	625 mL
Bottled lemon juice	1/3 cup	75 mL
Box of pectin crystals	2 oz.	57 g
Dried thyme	1/2 tsp.	2 mL
Pepper	1/2 tsp.	2 mL
Brown sugar, packed	4 cups	1 L

Combine first 4 ingredients in Dutch oven. Cook, covered, on medium for about 10 minutes, stirring occasionally, until onion is softened. Reduce heat to medium-low. Cook, uncovered, for about 25 minutes, stirring occasionally, until onion is caramelized.

Add next 5 ingredients. Bring to a boil, stirring constantly.

Add second amount of brown sugar. Bring to a hard boil, stirring constantly. Boil hard for 2 minutes, stirring constantly. Remove from heat. Stir for 5 minutes to suspend solids. Fill 4 hot sterilized 1 cup (250 mL) jars to within 1/4 inch (6 mm) of top. Remove air bubbles and adjust headspace if necessary. Wipe rims. Place hot metal lids on jars and screw on metal bands fingertip tight. Do not over-tighten. Process in boiling water bath for 20 minutes (see page 9). Remove jars. Let stand at room temperature until cool. If jam does not set the following day, let stand in a cool, dark place for 1 to 2 weeks until set. Makes about 4 2/3 cups (1.15 L).

1 tbsp. (15 mL): 60 Calories; 0 g Total Fat (0 g Mono, 0 g Poly, 0 g Sat); 0 mg Cholesterol; 13 g Carbohydrate; 0 g Fibre; 0 g Protein; 5 mg Sodium

Melon Lime Marmalade

This beautiful golden marmalade gets its mild sweetness from honeydew and a dose of zippy freshness from lime. Full of summery freshness, and delicious served on fresh, warm biscuits.

Small limes (see Tip, page 65)	5	5
Medium orange (see Tip, page 65)	1	1
Chopped honeydew	5 cups	1.25 L
Lime juice	1/3 cup	75 mL
Water	1/4 cup	60 mL
Box of pectin crystals	2 oz.	57 g
Granulated sugar	5 cups	1.25 L

Remove rind from limes and orange using vegetable peeler. Finely chop rind. Transfer to Dutch oven. Remove and discard pith from fruit. Segment fruit over pot to catch juices (see Tip, page 146). Finely chop segments. Add to pot.

Process next 3 ingredients in blender or food processor until smooth. Add to pot. Bring to a boil. Reduce heat to medium-low. Simmer, covered, for 15 minutes.

Add pectin. Bring to a boil, stirring constantly.

Add sugar. Bring to a hard boil, stirring constantly. Boil hard for 1 minute, stirring constantly. Remove from heat. Stir for 5 minutes to suspend solids. Fill 6 hot sterile 1 cup (250 mL) jars to within 1/4 inch (6 mm) of top. Remove air bubbles and adjust headspace if necessary. Wipe rims. Place hot metal lids on jars and screw on metal bands fingertip tight. Do not over-tighten. Process in boiling water bath for 15 minutes (see page 9). Remove jars. Let stand at room temperature until cool. If marmalade does not set the following day, let stand in a cool, dark place for 1 to 2 weeks until set. Makes about 6 1/2 cups (1.6 L).

1 tbsp. (15 mL): 45 Calories; 0 g Total Fat (0 g Mono, 0 g Poly, 0 g Sat); 0 mg Cholesterol; 11 g Carbohydrate; 0 g Fibre; 0 g Protein; 0 mg Sodium

Roasted Pepper Freezer Spread

Roasted red peppers with a kick of chili heat. It's hard to imagine a better combination. Serve this convenient freezer preserve with crackers and other dippers, or as a sandwich spread.

Large red peppers, halved	3	3
Medium onion, cut into wedges	1	1
Chopped walnuts, toasted (see Tip, page 50)	3/4 cup	175 mL
Fine dry bread crumbs	2/3 cup	150 mL
Lemon juice	3 tbsp.	45 mL
Liquid honey	1 tbsp.	15 mL
Tomato paste (see Tip, page 92)	1 tbsp.	15 mL
Garlic cloves, minced (or 1/2 tsp., 2 mL, powder)	2	2
Chili paste (sambal oelek)	2 tsp.	10 mL
Ground cumin	1 tsp.	5 mL
Salt	1/2 tsp.	2 mL
Olive (or cooking) oil	1/4 cup	60 mL

Place red pepper halves, cut-side down, and onion on greased baking sheet with sides. Broil on top rack in oven for about 15 minutes until pepper skins are blistered and blackened. Transfer onion to food processor. Transfer peppers to large bowl. Cover with plastic wrap. Let sweat for about 15 minutes until cool enough to handle. Remove and discard skins. Transfer peppers with juice to food processor.

Add next 9 ingredients. Process until coarsely chopped.

With motor running, slowly add olive oil in thin stream through hole in feed chute. Process until mixture is smooth. Fill clean plastic containers to within 1/2 inch (12 mm) of top (see Tip, page 79). Wipe rims. Cover with tight-fitting lids. Store in refrigerator for up to 2 weeks or in freezer for up to 3 months. Makes about 3 cups (750 mL).

1 tbsp. (15 mL): 35 Calories; 2.5 g Total Fat (1 g Mono, 1 g Poly, 0 g Sat); 0 mg Cholesterol; 3 g Carbohydrate; 0 g Fibre; trace Protein; 40 mg Sodium

Strawberry Pepper Vinegar

Sweet summery flavours, a rosy colour, and a little peppery kick bring out the very best in delicate summer greens.

Crushed fresh strawberries	1 cup	250 mL
Red wine vinegar	1 cup	250 mL
Whole black peppercorns	1/2 tsp.	2 mL
Port wine (optional)	2 tbsp.	30 mL

Combine first 3 ingredients in small glass bowl. Cover tightly with plastic wrap. Chill for 1 week, stirring every 2 to 3 days. Strain strawberry mixture through fine sieve or colander lined with 4 layers of damp cheesecloth into separate small glass bowl. Let stand in refrigerator overnight. Do not squeeze solids. Discard solids. Transfer liquid to small saucepan.

Add port. Stir. Heat on medium until hot, but not boiling. Fill 3 hot sterile 1/2 cup (125 mL) jars to within 1/4 inch (6 mm) of top. Wipe rims. Place hot metal lids on jars and screw on metal bands fingertip tight. Do not over-tighten. Process in boiling water bath for 15 minutes (see page 9). Remove jars. Let stand at room temperature until cool. Store in refrigerator for up to 2 weeks after opening. Makes about 1 1/3 cups (325 mL).

1 tbsp. (15 mL): 3 Calories; 0 g Total Fat (0 g Mono, 0 g Poly, 0 g Sat); 0 mg Cholesterol; trace Carbohydrate; 0 g Fibre; 0 g Protein; 0 mg Sodium

1. Strawberry Mango Freezer Jam, page 77

Gorgeous Green Pesto

Make this herbaceous pesto when the fresh ingredients are in season, inexpensive and plentiful. Freeze in tablespoonfuls on a baking sheet or in ice cube trays and then store in freezer bags to enjoy year round. Serve tossed with hot pasta, or added to sauces, stews, soups or vinaigrettes.

Fresh basil leaves, lightly packed	1 1/2 cups	375 mL
Fresh spinach leaves, lightly packed	1 1/2 cups	375 mL
Fresh parsley leaves, lightly packed	1 cup	250 mL
Grated Parmesan cheese	1/3 cup	75 mL
Salted, roasted shelled pumpkin seeds	1/3 cup	75 mL
Olive (or cooking) oil	1/4 cup	60 mL
Chopped fresh chives (or green onion)	3 tbsp.	45 mL
Balsamic vinegar	2 tbsp.	30 mL
Garlic clove, minced	1	1
Pepper	1/2 tsp.	2 mL
Salt	1/4 tsp.	1 mL

Process all 11 ingredients in food processor, scraping down sides if necessary, until smooth. Fill clean plastic containers to within 1/2 inch (12 mm) of top (see Tip, page 79). Wipe rims. Cover with tight-fitting lids. Store in refrigerator for up to 4 days or in freezer for up to 3 months. Makes about 1 1/3 cups (325 mL).

1 tbsp. (15 mL): 35 Calories; 3 g Total Fat (2 g Mono, 0 g Poly, 0.5 g Sat); 0 mg Cholesterol; 1 g Carbohydrate; 0 g Fibre; 1 g Protein; 60 mg Sodium

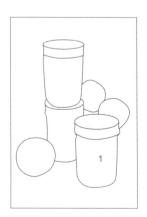

1. Nectarine Jam, page 76

Honey Apple Beer Mustard

*This thick, robust mustard has bold beer flavour, spicy kick and
an underlying sweetness that won't soon be forgotten. The perfect condiment
to have on hand at Oktoberfest.*

Dark beer (such as honey brown)	1 1/2 cups	375 mL
Brown mustard seed	1 cup	250 mL
Apple juice	1 cup	250 mL
Apple cider vinegar	1/2 cup	125 mL
Liquid honey	1/3 cup	75 mL
Dry mustard	1/4 cup	60 mL
Onion powder	1 tsp.	5 mL

Combine beer and mustard seed in large saucepan. Bring to a boil. Remove
from heat. Let stand, covered, for about 2 hours until liquid is absorbed.
Transfer to blender or food processor. Process until almost smooth. Mixture
should be grainy. Return to same saucepan.

Whisk in remaining 5 ingredients. Bring to a boil, stirring constantly. Reduce
heat to medium. Boil gently, uncovered, for about 25 minutes, stirring
often, until thickened. Fill 5 hot sterile 1/2 cup (125 mL) jars to within
1/4 inch (6 mm) of top. Remove air bubbles and adjust headspace if
necessary. Wipe rims. Place hot metal lids on jars and screw on metal
bands fingertip tight. Do not over-tighten. Process in boiling water bath
for 15 minutes (see page 9). Remove jars. Let stand at room temperature
until cool. Makes about 2 1/2 cups (625 mL).

*1 tsp. (5 mL): 10 Calories; 0 g Total Fat (0 g Mono, 0 g Poly, 0 g Sat); 0 mg Cholesterol;
1 g Carbohydrate; 0 g Fibre; 0 g Protein; 0 mg Sodium*

 tip   If a recipe calls for less than an entire can of tomato paste, freeze
the unopened can for 30 minutes. Open both ends and push the
contents through one end. Slice off only what you need. Freeze
the remaining paste in a resealable freezer bag or plastic wrap for
future use.

Fruit Ketchup

Grilled meats will never be the same. Lovely fruit flavours combine with tangy cider vinegar and mustard in this unique and fruity ketchup that makes a delicious condiment for turkey, chicken and pork.

Chopped dried apricot	2 cups	500 mL
Water	2 cups	500 mL
Chopped onion	1 cup	250 mL
Sultana raisins	1 cup	250 mL
Garlic cloves, chopped	3	3
Chopped seeded tomato	4 cups	1 L
Apple cider vinegar	1/2 cup	125 mL
Dry mustard	2 tsp.	10 mL
Salt	1 tsp.	5 mL
Pepper	1 tsp.	5 mL

Combine first 5 ingredients in large saucepan. Bring to a boil. Reduce heat to medium-low. Simmer, covered, for about 20 minutes, stirring occasionally, until fruit is very soft.

Add tomato. Stir. Carefully process in batches in food processor until smooth (see Safety Tip). Return to same saucepan.

Add remaining 4 ingredients. Stir. Bring to a boil, stirring constantly. Reduce heat to medium. Simmer, partially covered, for about 15 minutes, stirring occasionally, until thickened. Fill 5 hot sterile 1 cup (250 mL) jars to within 1/2 inch (12 mm) of top. Remove air bubbles and adjust headspace if necessary. Wipe rims. Place hot metal lids on jars and screw on metal bands fingertip tight. Do not over-tighten. Process in boiling water bath for 20 minutes (see page 9). Remove jars. Let stand at room temperature until cool. Makes about 6 cups (1.5 L).

1 tbsp. (15 mL): 15 Calories; 0 g Total Fat (0 g Mono, 0 g Poly, 0 g Sat); 0 mg Cholesterol; 4 g Carbohydrate; 0 g Fibre; 0 g Protein; 25 mg Sodium

Safety Tip: Follow manufacturer's instructions for processing hot liquids.

Raspberry Basil Vinegar

A pleasant vinegar infused with tart raspberry and a hint of basil. This vinegar makes a nice base for salad dressings and marinades, or mix a bit with yogurt and honey for a fruit dip with added punch.

Crushed fresh (or frozen, thawed) raspberries	1 cup	250 mL
White balsamic (or white wine) vinegar	1 cup	250 mL
Chopped fresh basil	2 tbsp.	30 mL

Combine all 3 ingredients in small glass bowl. Cover tightly with plastic wrap. Chill for 1 week, stirring every 2 to 3 days. Strain raspberry mixture through fine sieve or colander lined with 4 layers of damp cheesecloth into separate small glass bowl. Let stand in refrigerator overnight. Do not squeeze solids. Discard solids. Transfer liquid to small saucepan. Heat on medium until hot, but not boiling. Fill 3 hot sterile 1/2 cup (125 mL) jars to within 1/4 inch (6 mm) of top. Wipe rims. Place hot metal lids on jars and screw on metal bands fingertip tight. Do not over-tighten. Process in boiling water bath for 15 minutes (see page 9). Remove jars. Let stand at room temperature until cool. Store in refrigerator for up to 2 weeks after opening. Makes about 1 1/3 cups (325 mL).

1 tbsp. (15 mL): 10 Calories; 0 g Total Fat (0 g Mono, 0 g Poly, 0 g Sat); 0 mg Cholesterol; 2 g Carbohydrate; 0 g Fibre; 0 g Protein; 0 mg Sodium

 tip Chipotle chili peppers are smoked jalapeno peppers. Be sure to wash your hands after handling. To store any leftover chipotle peppers, divide into recipe-friendly portions and freeze, with sauce, in airtight containers for up to one year.

Red Pepper Chipotle Ketchup

This sweet roasted red pepper ketchup gets its fiery heat from chipotle peppers. Great on burgers and grilled meats, or with sweet potato fries. Or try adding some to a corn salsa for a healthy dose of spicy kick.

Large red peppers, halved	8	8
Chopped onion	2 cups	500 mL
Brown sugar, packed	1 1/3 cups	325 mL
Apple cider vinegar	1 cup	250 mL
Finely chopped chipotle peppers in adobo sauce (see Tip, page 94)	2 tbsp.	30 mL
Garlic cloves, chopped (or 3/4 tsp., 4 mL, powder)	3	3
Dry mustard	2 tsp.	10 mL
Ground cumin	1 tsp.	5 mL
Salt	1 tsp.	5 mL
Pepper	1/2 tsp.	2 mL

Place red pepper halves, cut-side down, on ungreased large baking sheet with sides. Broil on top rack in oven for about 10 minutes until skins are blistered and blackened. Transfer to large bowl. Cover with plastic wrap. Let sweat for about 15 minutes until cool enough to handle. Remove and discard skins. Coarsely chop. Transfer to large saucepan.

Add remaining 9 ingredients. Stir. Process in batches in blender until smooth. Return to same saucepan. Bring to a boil. Reduce heat to medium. Boil gently, uncovered, for about 30 minutes, stirring often, until thickened. Fill 6 hot sterile 1 cup (250 mL) jars to within 1/2 inch (12 mm) of top. Remove air bubbles and adjust headspace if necessary. Wipe rims. Place hot metal lids on jars and screw on metal bands fingertip tight. Do not over-tighten. Process in boiling water bath for 20 minutes (see page 9). Remove jars. Let stand at room temperature until cool. Makes about 6 cups (1.5 L).

1 tbsp. (15 mL): 15 Calories; 0 g Total Fat (0 g Mono, 0 g Poly, 0 g Sat); 0 mg Cholesterol; 4 g Carbohydrate; 0 g Fibre; 0 g Protein; 25 mg Sodium

Apricot Mustard

This traditional-style mustard has a nice grainy texture and plenty of mustardy bite. Apricot adds a touch of tangy sweetness to this unique condiment.

Water	2 cups	500 mL
Chopped dried apricot	1 1/4 cups	300 mL
Yellow mustard seed	1/2 cup	125 mL
Apple cider vinegar	2/3 cup	150 mL
Dry mustard	2 tbsp.	30 mL
Salt	1/2 tsp.	2 mL

Combine first 3 ingredients in small saucepan. Bring to a boil on medium. Reduce heat to medium-low. Simmer, uncovered, for about 15 minutes until apricot is softened. Carefully process in blender or food processor until almost smooth (see Safety Tip). Return to same saucepan.

Add remaining 3 ingredients. Heat and stir on medium until boiling. Fill 6 hot sterile 1/2 cup (125 mL) jars to within 1/4 inch (6 mm) of top. Remove air bubbles and adjust headspace if necessary. Wipe rims. Place hot metal lids on jars and screw on metal bands fingertip tight. Do not over-tighten. Process in boiling water bath for 15 minutes (see page 9). Remove jars. Let stand at room temperature until cool. Makes about 2 3/4 cups (675 mL).

1 tsp. (5 mL): 15 Calories; 0 g Total Fat (0 g Mono, 0 g Poly, 0 g Sat); 0 mg Cholesterol; 2 g Carbohydrate; 0 g Fibre; trace Protein; 10 mg Sodium

Safety Tip: Follow manufacturer's instructions for processing hot liquids.

Raspberry Peppercorn Mustard

This mildly sweetened mustard has subtle undertones of raspberry. This coarse, grainy-textured mustard has lots of peppery bite that mellows slightly as you let the mustard stand for a couple of weeks.

Dry white wine	1 cup	250 mL
Brown mustard seed	1/2 cup	125 mL
Yellow mustard seed	1/2 cup	125 mL
Raspberry vinegar	1 cup	250 mL
Liquid honey	1/2 cup	125 mL
Black peppercorns, crushed	2 tbsp.	30 mL
Salt	1/2 tsp.	2 mL

Combine first 3 ingredients in small saucepan. Bring to a boil, stirring occasionally. Remove from heat. Let stand, covered, for about 1 hour until liquid is absorbed. Transfer to food processor.

Add vinegar. Process until almost smooth. Mixture should be grainy. Transfer to same saucepan.

Add remaining 3 ingredients. Stir. Bring to a boil, stirring often. Reduce heat to medium. Cook for about 10 minutes, stirring often, until thickened. Fill 5 hot sterile 1/2 cup (125 mL) jars to within 1/4 inch (6 mm) of top. Remove air bubbles and adjust headspace if necessary. Wipe rims. Place hot metal lids on jars and screw on metal bands fingertip tight. Do not over-tighten. Process in boiling water bath for 15 minutes (see page 9). Remove jars. Let stand at room temperature until cool. Makes about 2 1/2 cups (625 mL).

1 tsp. (5 mL): 15 Calories; 0 g Total Fat (0 g Mono, 0 g Poly, 0 g Sat); 0 mg Cholesterol; 2 g Carbohydrate; 0 g Fibre; 0 g Protein; 10 mg Sodium

Tomatillo Peach Ketchup

This spiced condiment is made with tomatillos, a distant relative of tomatoes, and is definitely not your average ketchup! A mixture of sweet-tart flavours that's excellent with French fries, chicken or pork.

Cinnamon sticks (4 inches, 10 cm, each), broken up	2	2
Whole allspice	1 tsp.	5 mL
Whole cloves	1 tsp.	5 mL
Yellow mustard seed	1 tsp.	5 mL
Whole black peppercorns	1/2 tsp.	2 mL
Chopped tomatillos (see Note, page 43)	4 cups	1 L
Chopped peeled peach (see Tip, page 129)	2 cups	500 mL
Brown sugar, packed	1 cup	250 mL
Chopped green pepper	1 cup	250 mL
White vinegar	3/4 cup	175 mL
Chopped onion	2/3 cup	150 mL
Chopped fresh jalapeño pepper (see Tip, page 116)	1/4 cup	60 mL
Lime juice	1/4 cup	60 mL
Coarse (pickling) salt	2 tsp.	10 mL
Garlic clove, minced (or 1/4 tsp., 1 mL, powder)	1	1

Place first 5 ingredients in centre of double-layered square of cheesecloth. Tie with butcher's string.

Combine remaining 10 ingredients in large saucepan. Add cheesecloth bag. Stir. Bring to a boil, stirring occasionally. Reduce heat to medium-low. Simmer, covered, for about 20 minutes, stirring occasionally, until vegetables are tender. Remove and discard cheesecloth bag. Carefully process in batches in blender or food processor until smooth (see Safety Tip). Return to same saucepan. Bring to a boil. Reduce heat to medium. Boil gently, uncovered, for about 20 minutes, stirring often, until reduced and thickened. Fill 4 hot sterile 1 cup (250 mL) jars to within 1/2 inch (12 mm) of top. Remove air bubbles and adjust headspace if necessary. Wipe rims.

(continued on next page)

Place hot metal lids on jars and screw on metal bands fingertip tight. Do not over-tighten. Process in boiling water bath for 20 minutes (see page 9). Remove jars. Let stand at room temperature until cool. Makes about 4 cups (1 L).

1 tbsp. (15 mL): *20 Calories; 0 g Total Fat (0 g Mono, 0 g Poly, 0 g Sat); 0 mg Cholesterol; 5 g Carbohydrate; 0 g Fibre; 0 g Protein; 70 mg Sodium*

Safety Tip: Follow manufacturer's instructions for processing hot liquids.

Chili Garlic Vinegar

This flavoured vinegar provides a unique taste experience. First enjoy balsamic sweetness, followed by garlic, then a mild chili heat will follow. Serve drizzled over grilled vegetables, chicken or pork.

Garlic cloves, chopped	3	3
Dried crushed chilies	1 tsp.	5 mL
White balsamic (or white wine) vinegar	2 cups	500 mL

Combine garlic and chilies in sterile jar.

Bring vinegar to a boil in small saucepan. Carefully pour over garlic mixture in jar. Let stand until cool. Cover with tight-fitting lid. Chill for 1 week, gently shaking jar every 2 to 3 days. Strain through 4 layers of cheesecloth into small saucepan. Heat on medium until hot, but not boiling. Pour into 3 hot sterile 1/2 cup (125 mL) jars to within 1/4 inch (6 mm) of top. Wipe rims. Place hot metal lids on jars and screw on metal bands fingertip tight. Do not over-tighten. Process in boiling water bath for 15 minutes (see page 9). Remove jars. Let stand at room temperature until cool. Store in refrigerator for up to 2 weeks after opening. Makes about 1 3/4 cups (425 mL).

1 tbsp. (15 mL): *10 Calories; 0 g Total Fat (0 g Mono, 0 g Poly, 0 g Sat); 0 mg Cholesterol; 2 g Carbohydrate; 0 g Fibre; 0 g Protein; 0 mg Sodium*

Fig and Fennel Spread

If you're searching for a fine companion for serving with crackers and creamy cheeses, look no further. This thick spread is loaded with fennel flavour and a crunchy texture from the figs.

Chopped dried figs	1 cup	250 mL
Water	1 cup	250 mL
Chopped onion	1 1/2 cups	375 mL
White wine vinegar	2 tbsp.	30 mL
Liquid honey	1 tbsp.	15 mL
Fennel seed	1/2 tsp.	2 mL
Salt	1/2 tsp.	2 mL
Pepper	1/4 tsp.	1 mL
Chopped fennel bulb (white part only)	2 cups	500 mL

Combine figs and water in large saucepan. Bring to a boil. Reduce heat to medium-low. Cook, covered, for about 10 minutes until figs are softened. Transfer to food processor.

Add next 6 ingredients. Carefully process until smooth (see Safety Tip).

Add fennel. Process until fennel is finely chopped. Return to same saucepan. Bring to a boil, stirring occasionally. Reduce heat to medium. Cook, uncovered, for about 10 minutes, stirring often, until thickened. Fill clean plastic containers to within 1/2 inch (12 mm) of top (see Tip, page 79). Wipe rims. Let stand until cool. Cover with tight-fitting lids. Store in refrigerator for up to 2 weeks or in freezer for up to 3 months. Makes about 2 1/3 cups (575 mL).

1 tbsp. (15 mL): 15 Calories; 0 g Total Fat (0 g Mono, 0 g Poly, 0 g Sat); 0 mg Cholesterol; 4 g Carbohydrate; 0 g Fibre; 0 g Protein; 30 mg Sodium

Safety Tip: Follow manufacturer's instructions for processing hot liquids.

Pickled Green Tomatoes

Use up those end-of-season green tomatoes in these sweet, mildly spiced pickles.

Green tomatoes, cut into 1/2 inch (12 mm) wedges	3 1/2 lbs.	1.6 kg
Thinly sliced onion	1 cup	250 mL
Coarse (pickling) salt	3 tbsp.	45 mL
Apple cider vinegar	3 3/4 cups	925 mL
Brown sugar, packed	1 1/2 cups	375 mL
Pickling spice	2 tbsp.	30 mL

Combine first 3 ingredients in large bowl. Let stand, covered, at room temperature for 8 hours or overnight. Drain. Rinse with cold water. Drain well.

Combine vinegar and sugar in Dutch oven. Bring to a boil, stirring constantly. Add tomato mixture. Bring to a boil. Reduce heat to medium. Boil gently, uncovered, for 5 minutes, stirring occasionally, until heated through. Using slotted spoon, fill 4 hot sterile 2 cup (500 mL) jars with tomato mixture to within 1 inch (2.5 cm) of top.

Add pickling spice to hot vinegar mixture. Stir. Add to jars to within 1/2 inch (12 mm) of top. Discard any remaining vinegar mixture. Remove air bubbles and adjust headspace if necessary. Wipe rims. Place hot metal lids on jars and screw on metal bands fingertip tight. Do not over-tighten. Process in boiling water bath for 20 minutes (see page 9). Turn off heat. Let stand, uncovered, for 5 minutes. Remove jars. Let stand at room temperature until cool. Makes about 5 1/2 cups (1.4 L).

1/4 cup (60 mL): 90 Calories; 0 g Total Fat (0 g Mono, 0 g Poly, 0 g Sat); 0 mg Cholesterol; 19 g Carbohydrate; trace Fibre; trace Protein; 950 mg Sodium

Mixed Mustard Pickles

Bold mustard flavour in big, crisp pickles and red pepper slivers. These pickles come in a thick mustardy sauce that provides an interesting alternative to the usual pickle brine.

Sliced trimmed pickling cucumbers (1/4 inch, 6 mm, thick)	3 cups	750 mL
Cauliflower florets, halved	1 1/2 cups	375 mL
Sliced onion	1 1/2 cups	375 mL
Slivered red pepper	1 cup	250 mL
Coarse (pickling) salt	1/2 cup	125 mL
Water, to cover		
Granulated sugar	1 cup	250 mL
All-purpose flour	1/3 cup	75 mL
Dry mustard	2 tbsp.	30 mL
Mustard seed	2 tsp.	10 mL
Turmeric	1 1/2 tsp.	7 mL
Curry powder	1/2 tsp.	2 mL
Apple cider vinegar	1/2 cup	125 mL
Apple cider vinegar	2 1/2 cups	625 mL

Put first 4 ingredients into large bowl. Sprinkle with salt. Add water to cover. Stir. Chill, covered, for at least 6 hours or overnight. Drain. Rinse with cold water. Drain well.

Combine next 6 ingredients in medium bowl. Add first amount of vinegar. Stir until smooth.

Bring second amount of vinegar to a boil in Dutch oven. Add sugar mixture, whisking constantly until smooth. Reduce heat to medium. Heat and stir until boiling and thickened. Add cucumber mixture. Bring to a boil. Heat and stir for 5 minutes. Fill 3 hot sterile 2 cup (500 mL) jars to within 1/2 inch (12 mm) of top. Remove air bubbles and adjust headspace if necessary. Discard any remaining vinegar mixture. Wipe rims. Place hot metal lids on jars and screw on metal bands fingertip tight. Do not over-tighten. Process in boiling water bath for 15 minutes (see page 9). Turn off heat. Let stand, uncovered, for 5 minutes. Remove jars. Let stand at room temperature until cool. Makes about 6 1/2 cups (1.6 L).

1/4 cup (60 mL): 50 Calories; 0 g Total Fat (0 g Mono, 0 g Poly, 0 g Sat); 0 mg Cholesterol; 11 g Carbohydrate; 0 g Fibre; trace Protein; 2110 mg Sodium

Pickles

Ginger Beet Pickle

Pickled ginger is certainly pretty in pink with the addition of colourful beet.
A great condiment to keep on hand for serving with Japanese meals.

White vinegar	1 cup	250 mL
Rice vinegar	2/3 cup	150 mL
Grated peeled beet (see Tip, below)	1/2 cup	125 mL
Granulated sugar	1/3 cup	75 mL
Salt	2 tsp.	10 mL
Dried crushed chilies (optional)	1/4 tsp.	1 mL
Thinly sliced ginger root	1 1/2 cups	375 mL

Combine first 6 ingredients in medium saucepan. Bring to a boil, stirring constantly.

Add ginger. Reduce heat to medium-low. Simmer, uncovered, for 10 minutes to blend flavours. Using slotted spoon, fill 4 hot sterile 1/2 cup (125 mL) jars with ginger mixture to within 1 inch (2.5 cm) of top. Add hot vinegar mixture to jars to within 1/2 inch (12 mm) of top. Remove air bubbles and adjust headspace if necessary. Discard any remaining vinegar mixture. Wipe rims. Place hot metal lids on jars and screw on metal bands fingertip tight. Do not over-tighten. Process in boiling water bath for 15 minutes (see page 9). Turn off heat. Let stand, uncovered, for 5 minutes. Remove jars. Let stand at room temperature until cool. Makes about 1 3/4 cups (425 mL).

1/4 cup (60 mL): 80 Calories; 0 g Total Fat (0 g Mono, 0 g Poly, 0 g Sat); 0 mg Cholesterol; 19 g Carbohydrate; trace Fibre; trace Protein; 680 mg Sodium

Pictured on page 125.

 tip Don't get caught red-handed! Wear rubber gloves when handling beets.

Mr. Piper's Pepper Pickles

Yowza! This pretty mix of pickled peppers packs some potent heat! Use in sandwiches, as a pizza topping, or chopped and stirred into softened cream cheese for a zesty spread.

Sliced fresh banana pepper, with seeds (see Tip, page 116)	3 cups	750 mL
Sliced fresh jalapeño pepper, with seeds (see Tip, page 116)	2 1/2 cups	625 mL
Slivered orange pepper	2 1/2 cups	625 mL
White vinegar	4 cups	1 L
Water	1 cup	250 mL
Granulated sugar	1/3 cup	75 mL
Coarse (pickling) salt	1 tbsp.	15 mL
Garlic cloves, halved	2	2

Toss first 3 ingredients in large bowl. Pack pepper mixture into 4 hot sterile 2 cup (500 mL) jars to within 1 inch (2.5 cm) of top.

Combine remaining 5 ingredients in medium saucepan. Bring to a boil, stirring often. Reduce heat to medium-low. Simmer, uncovered, for 5 minutes to blend flavours. Remove and discard garlic. Add hot vinegar mixture to jars to within 1/2 inch (12 mm) of top. Remove air bubbles and adjust headspace if necessary. Discard any remaining vinegar mixture. Wipe rims. Place hot metal lids on jars and screw on metal bands fingertip tight. Do not over-tighten. Process in boiling water bath for 15 minutes (see page 9). Turn off heat. Let stand, uncovered, for 5 minutes. Remove jars. Let stand at room temperature until cool. Makes about 8 cups (2 L).

1/4 cup (60 mL): 20 Calories; 0 g Total Fat (0 g Mono, 0 g Poly, 0 g Sat); 0 mg Cholesterol; 5 g Carbohydrate; trace Fibre; 0 g Protein; 220 mg Sodium

Pickled Beets

Classic pickled beets with sweet spices adding depth to the flavour.

Unpeeled beets, scrubbed clean and trimmed (see Note)	3 lbs.	1.4 kg
Water, to cover		
Water	3 cups	750 mL
Raspberry vinegar	1 1/2 cups	375 mL
Granulated sugar	3/4 cup	175 mL
Coarse (pickling) salt	1 tbsp.	15 mL
Cinnamon stick (4 inches, 10 cm)	1	1
Whole allspice	1/4 tsp.	1 mL
Whole cloves	1/4 tsp.	1 mL

Put beets into Dutch oven. Add water to cover. Bring to a boil. Reduce heat to medium. Boil gently, covered, for about 45 minutes until tender.

Drain. Rinse beets with cold water. Remove and discard peels (see Tip, page 103). Cut beets into quarters. Cut quarters crosswise into 1/2 inch (12 mm) slices.

Combine remaining 7 ingredients in same Dutch oven. Bring to a boil, stirring occasionally. Reduce heat to medium-low. Simmer, covered, for 15 minutes. Add beets. Bring to a boil, stirring often. Using slotted spoon, fill 4 hot sterile 2 cup (500 mL) jars with beets to within 1 inch (2.5 cm) of top. Add hot vinegar mixture to within 1/2 inch (12 mm) of top. Remove air bubbles and adjust headspace if necessary. Discard any remaining vinegar mixture and solids. Wipe rims. Place hot metal lids on jars and screw on metal bands fingertip tight. Do not over-tighten. Process in boiling water bath for 35 minutes (see page 9). Turn off heat. Let stand, uncovered, for 5 minutes. Remove jars. Let stand at room temperature until cool. Makes about 8 cups (2 L).

1/4 cup (60 mL): 40 Calories; 0 g Total Fat (0 g Mono, 0 g Poly, 0 g Sat); 0 mg Cholesterol; 9 g Carbohydrate; trace Fibre; trace Protein; 250 mg Sodium

Note: To trim beets, leave root and 2 inches (5 cm) of stem intact.

Thai Pickled Carrots

Enjoy all your favourite Thai flavours of lemon grass, ginger, lime and hot peppers in these lovely pickled baby carrots. Crisp, sweet and with a nice dose of spicy heat.

Baby carrots, larger ones halved lengthwise	2 lbs.	900 g
Julienned ginger root (see Tip, page 47)	1/4 cup	60 mL
Sliced lemon grass, bulb only	1/4 cup	60 mL
Thai hot chili peppers, halved (see Tip, page 116)	2	2
White vinegar	2 1/2 cups	625 mL
Granulated sugar	1 1/4 cups	300 mL
Water	1 1/4 cups	300 mL
Lime juice	2/3 cup	150 mL
Coarse (pickling) salt	2 1/2 tsp.	12 mL

Pack 4 hot sterile 2 cup (500 mL) jars with carrots to within 1 inch (2.5 cm) of top. Add next 3 ingredients.

Combine remaining 5 ingredients in large saucepan. Bring to a boil, stirring often. Reduce heat to medium. Boil gently, uncovered, for 5 minutes. Add hot vinegar mixture to jars to within 1/2 inch (12 mm) of top. Remove air bubbles and adjust headspace if necessary. Wipe rims. Place hot metal lids on jars and screw on metal bands fingertip tight. Do not over-tighten. Process in boiling water bath for 15 minutes (see page 9). Turn off heat. Let stand, uncovered, for 5 minutes. Remove jars. Let stand at room temperature until cool. Makes about 6 cups (1.5 L).

1/4 cup (60 mL): 60 Calories; 0 g Total Fat (0 g Mono, 0 g Poly, 0 g Sat); 0 mg Cholesterol; 16 g Carbohydrate; trace Fibre; 0 g Protein; 270 mg Sodium

1. Mango Kiwi Freezer Jam, page 151

Pickled Plums

An interesting mix of sweet and savoury pickled flavours. Be sure to use firm, ripe plums for best results. Serve as a condiment with pork, ham or chicken. It also works well as a topping for French toast!

Sliced red (or black) plums (1/2 inch, 12 mm, thick)	7 cups	1.75 L
Granulated sugar	1 1/2 cups	375 mL
Raspberry vinegar	3/4 cup	175 mL
White vinegar	1/2 cup	125 mL
Water	1/4 cup	60 mL
Ground cinnamon	1/2 tsp.	2 mL
Whole cloves	1/4 tsp.	1 mL

Pack plum slices into 7 hot sterile 1 cup (250 mL) jars to within 1 inch (2.5 cm) of top.

Combine remaining 6 ingredients in medium saucepan. Bring to a boil, stirring often. Reduce heat to medium. Boil gently, uncovered, for 10 minutes. Add hot vinegar mixture to jars to within 1/2 inch (12 mm) of top. Remove air bubbles and adjust headspace if necessary. Discard any remaining vinegar mixture. Wipe rims. Place hot metal lids on jars and screw on metal bands fingertip tight. Do not over-tighten. Process in boiling water bath for 20 minutes (see page 9). Turn off heat. Let stand, uncovered, for 5 minutes. Remove jars. Let stand at room temperature until cool. Makes about 7 cups (1.75 L).

1/4 cup (60 mL): 60 Calories; 0 g Total Fat (0 g Mono, 0 g Poly, 0 g Sat); 0 mg Cholesterol; 16 g Carbohydrate; trace Fibre; 0 g Protein; 0 mg Sodium

1. Tomato Basil Sauce, page 131

Crispy Refrigerator Pickles

Just as the name says, these simple refrigerator pickles are nice and crispy. Red pepper provides an attractive colour contrast that adds to the appeal.

Sliced trimmed pickling cucumbers (1/4 inch, 6 mm, thick)	3 cups	750 mL
Thinly sliced onion	1/2 cup	125 mL
Thinly sliced red pepper	1/2 cup	125 mL
Water	1 cup	250 mL
White vinegar	1 cup	250 mL
Granulated sugar	1/2 cup	125 mL
Coarse (pickling) salt	4 tsp.	20 mL
Dill seed	4 tsp.	20 mL
Celery seed	1/2 tsp.	2 mL
Turmeric	1/8 tsp.	0.5 mL

Combine first 3 ingredients in large bowl.

Combine remaining 7 ingredients in medium saucepan. Bring to a boil, stirring often. Reduce heat to medium-low. Simmer, covered, for 10 minutes. Pour over cucumber mixture. Let stand, covered loosely with plastic wrap, for about 40 minutes until cool. Using slotted spoon, fill 2 sterile 2 cup (500 mL) jars with cucumber mixture to within 1 inch (2.5 cm) of top. Strain vinegar mixture through sieve into medium bowl. Spoon seed mixture into jars. Add hot vinegar mixture to cover. Discard any remaining vinegar mixture. Wipe rims. Cover with tight-fitting lids. Chill for 1 day before opening. Store in refrigerator for up to 3 weeks. Makes about 4 cups (1 L).

1/4 cup (60 mL): 35 Calories; 0 g Total Fat (0 g Mono, 0 g Poly, 0 g Sat); 0 mg Cholesterol; 9 g Carbohydrate; 0 g Fibre; 0 g Protein; 570 mg Sodium

Pictured on page 125.

Garlic-free Dills

For those who enjoy a classic dill pickle without the garlic. Crunchy and satisfying with a mild chili heat that builds.

Water	16 cups	4 L
Coarse (pickling) salt	1/2 cup	125 mL
Small pickling cucumbers, trimmed	7 lbs.	3.2 kg
Ice cubes	16 cups	4 L
Mustard seed	5 tbsp.	75 mL
Celery seed	10 tsp.	50 mL
Fresh heads of dill (or 7 tsp., 35 mL, dill seed)	5	5
Dried crushed chilies	2 1/2 tsp.	12 mL
Water	6 cups	1.5 L
White vinegar	5 cups	1.25 L
Coarse (pickling) salt	1/2 cup	125 mL
Granulated sugar	1/4 cup	60 mL
Mixed pickling spice, tied in double layer of cheesecloth	3 tbsp.	45 mL

Stir first amounts of water and salt in large bowl until salt is dissolved.

Layer cucumbers and ice in large stock pot or pail. Pour salt mixture over top. Place weighted plate over top to submerge cucumbers in salt mixture. Chill for 12 hours. Drain. Rinse with cold water. Drain well. Pack cucumbers into 5 hot sterile 4 cup (1 L) jars to within 1 inch (2.5 cm) of top.

Add next 4 ingredients to jars.

Combine remaining 5 ingredients in Dutch oven. Bring to a boil, stirring occasionally. Reduce heat to medium. Boil gently, covered, for 15 minutes. Remove and discard cheesecloth bag. Add hot vinegar mixture to jars to within 1/2 inch (12 mm) of top. Remove air bubbles and adjust headspace if necessary. Discard any remaining vinegar mixture. Wipe rims. Place hot metal lids on jars and screw on metal bands fingertip tight. Do not over-tighten. Process in boiling water bath for 20 minutes (see page 9). Turn off heat. Let stand, uncovered, for 5 minutes. Remove jars. Let stand at room temperature until cool. Makes about 20 cups (5 L).

1 pickle (approx. 1.6 oz., 45 g): 15 Calories; 0 g Total Fat (0 g Mono, 0 g Poly, 0 g Sat); 0 mg Cholesterol; 4 g Carbohydrate; 0 g Fibre; trace Protein; 1560 mg Sodium

Garlic Dill Sandwich Slices

These garlicky dills have a flavour that's far more complex than store-bought varieties. Perfect for stacking up on barbecued burgers or sandwiches. For best results, select cucumbers that are about the same height as your jars.

Coarsely chopped garlic cloves	1/3 cup	75 mL
Dill seed (or 5 fresh heads of dill)	10 tsp.	50 mL
Mustard seed	2 1/2 tsp.	12 mL
Whole black peppercorns	2 1/2 tsp.	12 mL
Bay leaves	5	5
Pickling cucumbers, trimmed and sliced lengthwise (1/4 inch, 6 mm, thick)	3 1/2 lbs.	1.6 kg
Water	4 cups	1 L
White vinegar	4 cups	1 L
Granulated sugar	3/4 cup	175 mL
Coarse (pickling) salt	1/2 cup	125 mL
Mixed pickling spice, tied in double layer of cheesecloth	3 tbsp.	45 mL

Divide first 5 ingredients into 5 hot sterile 2 cup (500 mL) jars. Pack cucumber slices into jars to within 1 inch (2.5 cm) of top.

Combine remaining 5 ingredients in Dutch oven. Bring to a boil, stirring occasionally. Reduce heat to medium. Boil gently, covered, for 15 minutes. Remove and discard cheesecloth bag. Add hot vinegar mixture to jars to within 1/2 inch (12 mm) of top. Remove air bubbles and adjust headspace if necessary. Discard any remaining vinegar mixture. Wipe rims. Place hot metal lids on jars and screw on metal bands fingertip tight. Do not over-tighten. Process in boiling water bath for 20 minutes (see page 9). Turn off heat. Let stand, uncovered, for 5 minutes. Remove jars. Let stand at room temperature until cool. Makes about 11 cups (2.75 L).

1/4 cup (60 mL): 25 Calories; 0 g Total Fat (0 g Mono, 0 g Poly, 0 g Sat); 0 mg Cholesterol; 7 g Carbohydrate; 0 g Fibre; 0 g Protein; 1240 mg Sodium

Spicy Zucchini Pickles

These zucchini pickles may look like ordinary sweet pickles, though don't be fooled. There's plenty of spicy heat packed into these jars. Fans of hot chilies and ginger are sure to love these!

Sliced trimmed small zucchini (with peel), about 1 3/4 lbs. (790 g)	8 cups	2 L
Coarse (pickling) salt	1/3 cup	75 mL
Ice water, to cover	8 cups	2 L
White vinegar	2 cups	500 mL
Rice vinegar	1 cup	250 mL
Granulated sugar	1 1/2 cups	375 mL
Sliced fresh hot red chili pepper (see Tip, page 116)	3 tbsp.	45 mL
Chopped ginger root	3 tsp.	15 mL

Layer zucchini slices and salt in extra-large bowl. Add ice water to cover. Let stand, covered, at room temperature for 3 hours. Drain. Rinse with cold water. Drain well.

Combine next 3 ingredients in large saucepan. Bring to a boil, stirring constantly. Add zucchini. Bring to a boil, stirring occasionally. Remove from heat. Using slotted spoon, fill 3 hot sterile 2 cup (500 mL) jars with zucchini to within 1 inch (2.5 cm) of top.

Add chili pepper and ginger root to jars. Add hot vinegar mixture to within 1/2 inch (12 mm) of top. Remove air bubbles and adjust headspace if necessary. Wipe rims. Discard any remaining vinegar mixture. Place hot metal lids on jars and screw on metal bands fingertip tight. Do not over-tighten. Process in boiling water bath for 15 minutes (see page 9). Turn off heat. Let stand, uncovered, for 5 minutes. Remove jars. Let stand at room temperature until cool. Makes about 6 cups (1.5 L).

1/4 cup (60 mL): 60 Calories; 0 g Total Fat (0 g Mono, 0 g Poly, 0 g Sat); 0 mg Cholesterol; 16 g Carbohydrate; 0 g Fibre; 0 g Protein; 1520 mg Sodium

Tangy Bread and Butter Pickles

These bread and butter pickles are a touch spicier than the traditional ones. If you prefer a milder version, replace the jalapeño peppers with slivered red pepper and omit the dried crushed chilies.

Thinly sliced trimmed pickling cucumbers	8 cups	2 L
Thinly sliced sweet onion	3 cups	750 mL
Slivered red pepper	1 1/2 cups	375 mL
Thinly sliced fresh jalapeño pepper (see Tip, page 116)	1/2 cup	125 mL
Coarse (pickling) salt	3/4 cup	175 mL
Ice cubes	4 cups	1 L
Apple cider vinegar	3 cups	750 mL
Granulated sugar	3/4 cup	175 mL
Liquid honey	3/4 cup	175 mL
Mustard seed	1 tbsp.	15 mL
Celery seed	1 tsp.	5 mL
Dried crushed chilies	1/2 tsp.	2 mL
Turmeric	1/2 tsp.	2 mL

Toss first 5 ingredients in large bowl. Scatter ice cubes over top. Let stand, covered, at room temperature for 3 hours. Drain. Rinse with cold water. Drain well.

Combine remaining 7 ingredients in Dutch oven. Bring to a boil, stirring constantly. Add cucumber mixture. Stir. Bring to a boil. Using slotted spoon, fill 4 hot sterile 2 cup (500 mL) jars with cucumber mixture to within 1 inch (2.5 cm) of top. Add hot vinegar mixture to jars to within 1/2 inch (12 mm) of top. Remove air bubbles and adjust headspace if necessary. Discard any remaining vinegar mixture. Wipe rims. Place hot metal lids on jars and screw on metal bands fingertip tight. Do not over-tighten. Process in boiling water bath for 15 minutes (see page 9). Turn off heat. Let stand, uncovered, for 5 minutes. Remove jars. Let stand at room temperature until cool. Makes about 8 cups (2 L).

1/4 cup (60 mL): 60 Calories; 0 g Total Fat (0 g Mono, 0 g Poly, 0 g Sat); 0 mg Cholesterol; 14 g Carbohydrate; trace Fibre; 0 g Protein; 2570 mg Sodium

English Brown Pickle

Though this may not be what comes to mind when many people think of pickles, this savoury relish-like condiment is a pub staple in England. Try it with cheese and deli meats, or with bangers and mash.

Diced carrot	1 1/2 cups	375 mL
Diced yellow turnip (rutabaga)	1 1/2 cups	375 mL
Malt vinegar	1 1/3 cups	325 mL
Chopped onion	1 cup	250 mL
Dark beer	1 cup	250 mL
Diced peeled tart apple (such as Granny Smith)	1 cup	250 mL
Diced zucchini (with peel)	1 cup	250 mL
Chopped pitted dates	1/2 cup	125 mL
Dark brown sugar, packed	1/2 cup	125 mL
Bottled lemon juice	2 tbsp.	30 mL
Worcestershire sauce	1 tbsp.	15 mL
Garlic cloves, minced (or 1/2 tsp., 2 mL, powder)	2	2
Ground allspice	1 tsp.	5 mL
Salt	1 tsp.	5 mL
Yellow mustard seed	1 tsp.	5 mL
Cayenne pepper	1/8 tsp.	0.5 mL

Combine all 16 ingredients in large saucepan or Dutch oven. Bring to a boil on medium, stirring often. Reduce heat to medium-low. Simmer, uncovered, for about 75 minutes, stirring often, until turnip is tender but firm and mixture is thickened. Fill 4 hot sterile 1 cup (250 mL) jars to within 1/2 inch (12 mm) of top. Remove air bubbles and adjust headspace if necessary. Wipe rims. Place hot metal lids on jars and screw on metal bands fingertip tight. Do not over-tighten. Process in boiling water bath for 20 minutes (see page 9). Turn off heat. Let stand, uncovered, for 5 minutes. Remove jars. Let stand at room temperature until cool. Makes about 3 2/3 cups (900 mL).

1 tbsp. (15 mL): 20 Calories; 0 g Total Fat (0 g Mono, 0 g Poly, 0 g Sat); 0 mg Cholesterol; 5 g Carbohydrate; 0 g Fibre; 0 g Protein; 50 mg Sodium

Freezer Coleslaw

Looking for a simple side dish that you can stow away in your freezer for a later day? This crunchy coleslaw fits the bill. It can also be used as a condiment on corned beef (or other) sandwiches.

Shredded cabbage (or coleslaw mix), lightly packed	8 cups	2 L
Coarsely grated carrot, lightly packed	2 cups	500 mL
Slivered red pepper	1 cup	250 mL
Thinly sliced onion	1/2 cup	125 mL
Coarse (pickling) salt	3 tbsp.	45 mL
Apple cider vinegar	3 cups	750 mL
Granulated sugar	2 1/4 cups	550 mL
Celery seed	1 tbsp.	15 mL
Dried crushed chilies	1/2 tsp.	2 mL

Combine first 5 ingredients in large bowl. Chill, covered, for 8 hours or overnight. Drain. Rinse with cold water. Drain well. Squeeze cabbage mixture to remove excess moisture. Spread on paper towel-lined baking sheets. Blot dry. Fill clean plastic containers with cabbage mixture to within 1 inch (2.5 cm) of top (see Tip, page 79).

Combine remaining 4 ingredients in medium saucepan. Bring to a boil, stirring often until sugar is dissolved. Pour hot vinegar mixture over cabbage mixture to within 1/2 inch (12 mm) of top. Wipe rims. Let stand until cool. Cover with tight-fitting lids. Store in refrigerator for up to 2 weeks or in freezer for up to 2 months. Makes about 5 1/2 cups (1.4 L).

1/4 cup (60 mL): 100 Calories; 0 g Total Fat (0 g Mono, 0 g Poly, 0 g Sat); 0 mg Cholesterol; 24 g Carbohydrate; 1 g Fibre; trace Protein; 950 mg Sodium

 tip Hot peppers contain capsaicin in the seeds and ribs. Removing the seeds and ribs will reduce the heat. Wear rubber gloves when handling hot peppers and avoid touching your eyes and nose. Wash your hands well afterwards.

Pickled Garlic

The perfect preserve for those with a serious love for garlic. Serve sliced cloves in a salad, add to an antipasto plate, or use as a garnish for a martini. Young garlic cloves may discolour slightly in the brine, but it won't affect the taste.

Water	8 cups	2 L
Unpeeled garlic cloves (see Note)	4 cups	1 L
White vinegar	1 1/2 cups	375 mL
Dry vermouth	1/2 cup	125 mL
Granulated sugar	2 tbsp.	30 mL
Coarse (pickling) salt	1 tbsp.	15 mL

Bring water to a boil in Dutch oven. Add garlic. Boil for 1 minute. Drain. Rinse with cold water. Remove and discard skins. Discard any cloves with blemishes. Pack garlic into 4 hot sterile 1 cup (250 mL) jars to within 1 inch (2.5 cm) of top.

Combine remaining 4 ingredients in medium saucepan. Bring to a boil, stirring constantly. Reduce heat to medium-low. Simmer, covered, for 5 minutes. Add hot vinegar mixture to jars to within 1/2 inch (12 mm) of top. Remove air bubbles and adjust headspace if necessary. Discard any remaining vinegar mixture. Wipe rims. Place hot metal lids on jars and screw on metal bands fingertip tight. Do not over-tighten. Process in boiling water bath for 15 minutes (see page 9). Turn off heat. Let stand, uncovered, for 5 minutes. Remove jars. Let stand at room temperature until cool. Makes about 4 cups (1 L).

2 tbsp. (30 mL): 30 Calories; 0 g Total Fat (0 g Mono, 0 g Poly, 0 g Sat); 0 mg Cholesterol; 7 g Carbohydrate; 0 g Fibre; 1 g Protein; 210 mg Sodium

Note: Do not use garlic cloves with green stems as these cloves will discolour during the pickling process.

Pickled Curried Onions

Sweet pickled onions with a vibrant golden colour and distinct curry flavour. A nice, colourful addition to a tray of assorted pickles.

Water	8 cups	2 L
Pearl onions, root ends trimmed and scored with an 'X'	4 1/2 cups	1.1 L
Garlic cloves, sliced	4	4
Chopped ginger root	1/4 cup	60 mL
White vinegar	2 cups	500 mL
Granulated sugar	1 1/2 cups	375 mL
Water	1/2 cup	125 mL
Coarse (pickling) salt	1 tbsp.	15 mL
Cumin seed	2 tsp.	10 mL
Coriander seed	1 tsp.	5 mL
Dried crushed chilies	1 tsp.	5 mL
Turmeric	1/2 tsp.	2 mL

Bring water to a boil in Dutch oven. Add onions. Boil for 1 minute. Drain. Plunge into cold water. Remove and discard skins.

Pack garlic, ginger and onions into 4 hot sterile 1 cup (250 mL) jars to within 1 inch (2.5 cm) of top.

Combine remaining 8 ingredients in medium saucepan. Bring to a boil, stirring often. Reduce heat to medium. Boil gently, covered, for 5 minutes. Add hot vinegar mixture to jars to within 1/2 inch (12 mm) of top. Remove air bubbles and adjust headspace if necessary. Discard any remaining vinegar mixture. Wipe rims. Place hot metal lids on jars and screw on metal bands fingertip tight. Do not over-tighten. Process in boiling water bath for 15 minutes (see page 9). Turn off heat. Let stand, uncovered, for 5 minutes. Remove jars. Let stand at room temperature until cool. Makes about 4 cups (1 L).

1/4 cup (60 mL): 90 Calories; 0 g Total Fat (0 g Mono, 0 g Poly, 0 g Sat); 0 mg Cholesterol; 24 g Carbohydrate; 1 g Fibre; trace Protein; 430 mg Sodium

Lemon Garden Pickle Mix

These colourful pickles have a decidedly cheerful appearance through the addition of lemon slices. Sweet and tangy with plenty of garden goodness. Use small zucchini for best results.

White vinegar	2 1/4 cups	550 mL
Granulated sugar	1 1/2 cups	375 mL
Lemon juice	3/4 cup	175 mL
Garlic cloves, sliced	4	4
Coarse (pickling) salt	1 tbsp.	15 mL
Whole black peppercorns	1 tbsp.	15 mL
Celery seed	2 tsp.	10 mL
Mustard seed	2 tsp.	10 mL
Whole allspice	1 tsp.	5 mL
Sliced trimmed small zucchini (with peel)	6 cups	1.5 L
Sliced carrot	2 cups	500 mL
Chopped onion	1 cup	250 mL
Chopped red pepper	1 cup	250 mL
Lemon slices, halved	8	8

Combine first 9 ingredients in Dutch oven or large pot. Bring to a boil, stirring constantly. Reduce heat to medium. Boil gently, covered, for 5 minutes.

Add next 4 ingredients. Stir. Bring to a boil. Remove from heat.

Put lemon slices into 4 hot sterile 2 cup (500 mL) jars. Using slotted spoon, add zucchini mixture to within 1 inch (2.5 cm) of top. Add hot vinegar mixture to jars to within 1/2 inch (12 mm) of top. Remove air bubbles and adjust head space if necessary. Discard any remaining vinegar mixture. Wipe rims. Place hot metal lids on jars and screw on metal bands fingertip tight. Do not over-tighten. Process in boiling water bath for 20 minutes (see page 9). Turn off heat. Let stand, uncovered, for 5 minutes. Remove jars. Let stand at room temperature until cool. Makes about 6 1/2 cups (1.6 L).

1/4 cup (60 mL): 70 Calories; 0 g Total Fat (0 g Mono, 0 g Poly, 0 g Sat); 0 mg Cholesterol; 17 g Carbohydrate; 1 g Fibre; trace Protein; 270 mg Sodium

Pictured on page 72.

Pickled Fruit Salad

Enjoy the natural flavours of pineapple and cantaloupe in this sweet and tangy blend of fruit and spices. Enjoy it as is, or chop finely to make a relish or salsa for serving with pork or turkey.

Granulated sugar	3 cups	750 mL
Red wine vinegar	2 cups	500 mL
Water	1 cup	250 mL
Chopped ginger root	1/4 cup	60 mL
Cinnamon sticks (4 inches, 10 cm, each)	2	2
Coarse (pickling) salt	1 tsp.	5 mL
Ground allspice	1/4 tsp.	1 mL
Ground cloves	1/4 tsp.	1 mL
Cubed cantaloupe (3/4 inch, 2 cm, pieces)	4 cups	1 L
Cubed fresh pineapple (3/4 inch, 2 cm, pieces)	4 cups	1 L

Combine first 8 ingredients in Dutch oven. Bring to a boil, stirring often. Reduce heat to medium-low. Simmer, covered, for 15 minutes. Remove and discard cinnamon sticks.

Add cantaloupe and pineapple. Cook, uncovered, for about 10 minutes, stirring often, until heated through. Using slotted spoon, fill 4 hot sterile 2 cup (500 mL) jars with fruit to within 1 inch (2.5 cm) of top. Add hot vinegar mixture to jars to within 1/2 inch (12 mm) of top. Remove air bubbles and adjust headspace if necessary. Discard any remaining vinegar mixture. Wipe rims. Place hot metal lids on jars and screw on metal bands fingertip tight. Do not over-tighten. Process in boiling water bath for 25 minutes (see page 9). Turn off heat. Let stand, uncovered, for 5 minutes. Remove jars. Let stand at room temperature until cool. Makes about 8 cups (2 L).

1/4 cup (60 mL): 90 Calories; 0 g Total Fat (0 g Mono, 0 g Poly, 0 g Sat); 0 mg Cholesterol; 23 g Carbohydrate; 0 g Fibre; 0 g Protein; 80 mg Sodium

Pickled Pumpkin

Not all pumpkins were destined to become jack-o-lanterns. This unique and delicious application for pumpkin has a fantastic taste and texture that you might not expect. Serve as a snack, or alongside roast turkey or chicken.

Granulated sugar	5 1/2 cups	1.4 L
Apple cider vinegar	2 cups	500 mL
White vinegar	3/4 cup	175 mL
Coarse (pickling) salt	1 tbsp.	15 mL
Cinnamon stick (4 inch, 10 cm)	1	1
Ground nutmeg	1/8 tsp.	0.5 mL
Cubed pumpkin (3/4 inch, 2 cm, pieces)	10 cups	2.5 L

Combine first 6 ingredients in Dutch oven. Bring to a boil, stirring constantly. Reduce heat to medium. Boil gently, uncovered, for 10 minutes.

Add pumpkin. Cook, uncovered, for about 10 minutes, stirring occasionally, until heated through. Remove and discard cinnamon stick. Using slotted spoon, fill 5 hot sterile 2 cup (500 mL) jars with pumpkin to within 1 inch (2.5 cm) of top. Add hot vinegar mixture to jars to within 1/2 inch (12 mm) of top. Remove air bubbles and adjust headspace if necessary. Discard any remaining vinegar mixture. Wipe rims. Place hot metal lids on jars and screw on metal bands fingertip tight. Do not over-tighten. Process in boiling water bath for 25 minutes (see page 9). Turn off heat. Let stand, uncovered, for 5 minutes. Remove jars. Let stand at room temperature until cool. Makes about 10 cups (2.5 L).

1/4 cup (60 mL): 120 Calories; 0 g Total Fat (0 g Mono, 0 g Poly, 0 g Sat); 0 mg Cholesterol; 30 g Carbohydrate; 0 g Fibre; 0 g Protein; 170 mg Sodium

Carrot Daikon Pickles

Add a little flair to an ordinary meal with this spicy mixture of pickled carrots and daikon radish. A great accompaniment for Japanese or Korean cuisine, or use as a unique garnish for a martini.

Sliced baby carrots (1/2 inch, 12 mm, thick)	2 cups	500 mL
Cubed daikon radish (1/2 inch, 12 mm, pieces)	1 1/2 cups	375 mL
White vinegar	1 1/2 cups	375 mL
Granulated sugar	1 cup	250 mL
Water	1/2 cup	125 mL
Mustard seed	1 tbsp.	15 mL
Coarse (pickling) salt	1 1/2 tsp.	7 mL
Dried crushed chilies	1 tsp.	5 mL

Arrange carrot and daikon in alternating layers in sterile 4 cup (1 L) jar.

Combine remaining 6 ingredients in large saucepan. Bring to a boil, stirring constantly. Reduce heat to medium. Boil gently, uncovered, for 5 minutes. Pour over vegetables to cover. Discard any remaining vinegar mixture. Wipe rim. Let stand until cool. Cover with tight-fitting lid. Chill for 1 day before opening. Store in refrigerator for up to 2 weeks. Makes about 4 cups (1 L).

1/4 cup (60 mL): 60 Calories; 0 g Total Fat (0 g Mono, 0 g Poly, 0 g Sat); 0 mg Cholesterol; 15 g Carbohydrate; trace Fibre; 0 g Protein; 230 mg Sodium

Grand Cranberry Sauce

Ordinary cranberry sauce just won't measure up to this fragrant and mildly spiced version. If you'd rather keep the sauce alcohol-free, just use an equal amount of orange juice instead.

Fresh (or frozen) cranberries	8 cups	2 L
Granulated sugar	2 cups	500 mL
Water	1/2 cup	125 mL
Ginger root slices, 1/8 inch (3 mm) thick	4	4
Orange slices, 1/4 inch (6 mm) thick	3	3
Cinnamon stick (4 inches, 10 cm)	1	1
Orange liqueur	1/2 cup	125 mL

Combine first 6 ingredients in large saucepan. Bring to a boil, stirring constantly. Reduce heat to medium-low. Simmer, uncovered, for about 15 minutes, stirring occasionally, until cranberries burst and mixture is thickened. Remove and discard ginger slices, orange slices and cinnamon stick.

Stir in liqueur. Fill 5 hot sterile 1 cup (250 mL) jars to within 1/2 inch (12 mm) of top. Remove air bubbles and adjust headspace if necessary. Wipe rims. Place hot metal lids on jars and screw on metal bands fingertip tight. Do not over-tighten. Process in boiling water bath for 20 minutes (see page 9). Remove jars. Let stand at room temperature until cool. Makes about 5 cups (1.25 L).

2 tbsp. (30 mL): 50 Calories; 0 g Total Fat (0 g Mono, 0 g Poly, 0 g Sat); 0 mg Cholesterol; 13 g Carbohydrate; trace Fibre; 0 g Protein; 0 mg Sodium

Lemon Mint Syrup

A must-try for mint enthusiasts. Goes great with ice cream, fruit, cocktails, iced tea, lemonade, waffles, crepes or French toast. For an interesting variation, use lime juice in place of lemon to make a mojito syrup!

Granulated sugar	2 cups	500 mL
Water	1 cup	250 mL
Fresh lemon juice	1/2 cup	125 mL
Fresh mint leaves, lightly packed	1/2 cup	125 mL

Combine all 4 ingredients in small saucepan. Bring to a boil, stirring often. Reduce heat to medium. Boil gently, uncovered, for about 10 minutes until thickened to a syrup consistency. Carefully strain through fine sieve into small bowl. Discard solids. Fill 4 hot sterile 1/2 cup (125 mL) jars to within 1/4 inch (6 mm) of top. Wipe rims. Place hot metal lids on jars and screw on metal bands fingertip tight. Do not over-tighten. Process in boiling water bath for 15 minutes (see page 9). Remove jars. Let stand at room temperature until cool. Makes about 2 cups (500 mL).

1 tbsp. (15 mL): *50 Calories; 0 g Total Fat (0 g Mono, 0 g Poly, 0 g Sat); 0 mg Cholesterol; 12 g Carbohydrate; 0 g Fibre; 0 g Protein; 0 mg Sodium*

1. Ginger Beet Pickle, page 103
2. Crispy Refrigerator Pickles, page 110

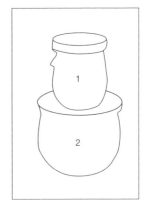

Peach Vanilla Sauce

This versatile sauce is perfect for preserving the flavour of fresh peaches while they're in season. Serve as a topping for sundaes, stirred into fruit salad, or spooned over angel food cake.

Chopped peeled peach (see Tip, page 129)	10 cups	2.5 L
Granulated sugar	1 cup	250 mL
Corn syrup	1/2 cup	125 mL
Vanilla bean	1	1
Bottled lemon juice	1 tsp.	5 mL

Combine first 3 ingredients in Dutch oven.

Split vanilla bean lengthwise. Scrape seeds from bean into peach mixture. Add vanilla bean halves. Stir. Bring to a boil. Reduce heat to medium-low. Cook, covered, for about 15 minutes, stirring occasionally, until peach is tender. Remove and discard vanilla bean halves. Carefully process with hand blender or in blender in batches until smooth (see Safety Tip).

Stir in lemon juice. Fill clean plastic containers to within 1/2 inch (12 mm) of top (see Tip, page 79). Wipe rims. Let stand at room temperature until cool. Cover with tight-fitting lids. Store in refrigerator for up to 1 week or in freezer for up to 2 months. Makes about 7 1/4 cups (1.8 L).

2 tbsp. (30 mL): 45 Calories; 0 g Total Fat (0 g Mono, 0 g Poly, 0 g Sat); 0 mg Cholesterol; 11 g Carbohydrate; 0 g Fibre; 0 g Protein; 5 mg Sodium

Safety Tip: Follow manufacturer's instructions for processing hot liquids.

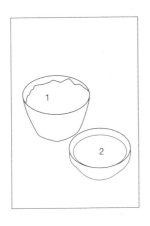

1. Curry Mango Jelly, page 82
2. Sweet Chili Sauce, page 130

Peach Plum Sauce

A sweet, fruitier take on plum sauce that stays true to the flavour you love.
So much better than store-bought!

Coarsely chopped black (or red) plums	2 cups	500 mL
Coarsely chopped peeled peach (see Tip, page 129)	1 1/2 cups	375 mL
Coarsely chopped onion	1/2 cup	125 mL
Finely grated ginger root (or 1/4 tsp., 1 mL, ground ginger)	1 tsp.	5 mL
Garlic clove, chopped (or 1/4 tsp., 1 mL, powder)	1	1
Brown sugar, packed	1 1/2 cups	375 mL
Apple cider vinegar	3/4 cup	175 mL
Salt	1/2 tsp.	2 mL
Ground cinnamon	1/4 tsp.	1 mL
Dried crushed chilies	1/8 tsp.	0.5 mL
Ground allspice	1/8 tsp.	0.5 mL
Ground cloves	1/8 tsp.	0.5 mL

Process first 5 ingredients in food processor until smooth. Transfer to large saucepan.

Add remaining 7 ingredients. Stir. Bring to a boil, stirring occasionally. Reduce heat to medium-low. Simmer, uncovered, for about 45 minutes, stirring often, until thickened. Fill 7 hot sterile 1/2 cup (125 mL) jars to within 1/2 inch (12 mm) of top. Remove air bubbles and adjust headspace if necessary. Wipe rims. Place hot metal lids on jars and screw on metal bands fingertip tight. Do not over-tighten. Process in boiling water bath for 15 minutes (see page 9). Remove jars. Let stand at room temperature until cool. Makes about 2 3/4 cups (675 mL).

2 tbsp. (30 mL): 70 Calories; 0 g Total Fat (0 g Mono, 0 g Poly, 0 g Sat); 0 mg Cholesterol; 18 g Carbohydrate; 0 g Fibre; 0 g Protein; 60 mg Sodium

Razz-Berry Syrup

A flavourful sweet-tart syrup enhanced by a touch of lemon. This colourful drizzle is great for serving over vanilla ice cream, waffles or pancakes. It also makes a great gift!

Fresh (or frozen) raspberries	11 cups	2.75 L
Water	1 cup	250 mL
Granulated sugar	3 cups	750 mL
Bottled lemon juice	1/4 cup	60 mL

Combine raspberries and water in Dutch oven. Bring to a boil, stirring occasionally. Reduce heat to medium. Boil gently, uncovered, for about 5 minutes, crushing occasionally with potato masher, until softened. Remove from heat. Carefully strain through fine sieve or colander lined with double layer of damp cheesecloth into large bowl. Let stand for 2 hours. Do not squeeze solids. Discard solids. Measure 4 cups (1 L) juice into large saucepan.

Add sugar and lemon juice. Stir. Bring to a boil, stirring constantly until sugar is dissolved. Reduce heat to medium-low. Simmer, uncovered, for 20 minutes, stirring occasionally. Skim and discard foam. Fill 5 hot sterile 1 cup (250 mL) jars to within 1/4 inch (6 mm) of top. Wipe rims. Place hot metal lids on jars and screw on metal bands fingertip tight. Do not over-tighten. Process in boiling water bath for 15 minutes (see page 9). Remove jars. Let stand at room temperature until cool. Makes about 5 cups (1.25 L).

1 tbsp. (15 mL): 35 Calories; 0 g Total Fat (0 g Mono, 0 g Poly, 0 g Sat); 0 mg Cholesterol; 9 g Carbohydrate; trace Fibre; 0 g Protein; 0 mg Sodium

Pictured on page 71.

 tip To peel fresh fruit and produce more easily, blanch in boiling water for 30 to 60 seconds. Immediately plunge into cold water and remove skins.

Sweet Chili Sauce

If store-bought chili sauces just aren't doing it anymore, this recipe is just what you're looking for. Experiment with different varieties of chili peppers to vary the heat. Add to stir-fries, or brush over grilled meats and fish, or use as a condiment with salad rolls.

Water	1/2 cup	125 mL
Chopped fresh hot red chili pepper (see Tip, page 116)	1/3 cup	75 mL
Garlic cloves, minced	4	4
Granulated sugar	2 cups	500 mL
Rice vinegar	1 1/2 cups	375 mL
White corn syrup	1/2 cup	125 mL
Salt	1/2 tsp.	2 mL

Combine first 3 ingredients in large saucepan. Bring to a boil. Reduce heat to medium-low. Simmer, covered, for about 5 minutes until chili pepper is softened. Carefully process in blender or food processor until almost smooth (see Safety Tip). Return to pot.

Add sugar and vinegar. Stir. Bring to a boil, stirring occasionally. Reduce heat to medium. Boil gently, uncovered, for about 15 minutes, stirring occasionally, until thickened to a syrup consistency.

Add corn syrup and salt. Stir. Bring to a boil. Boil gently for 5 minutes, stirring occasionally. Fill 5 hot sterilized 1/2 cup (125 mL) jars to within 1/2 inch (12 mm) of top. Wipe rims. Place hot metal lids on jars and screw on metal bands fingertip tight. Do not over-tighten. Process in boiling water bath for 20 minutes (see page 9). Remove jars. Let stand at room temperature until cool. Makes about 2 1/2 cups (625 mL).

1 tbsp. (15 mL): 50 Calories; 0 g Total Fat (0 g Mono, 0 g Poly, 0 g Sat); 0 mg Cholesterol; 14 g Carbohydrate; 0 g Fibre; 0 g Protein; 35 mg Sodium

Pictured on page 126.

Safety Tip: Follow manufacturer's instructions for processing hot liquids.

Tomato Basil Sauce

A bright, fresh-tasting sauce with traditional flavours. A great way to use your garden herbs and tomatoes so you can enjoy the flavour all year long. Serve over pasta with freshly grated cheese.

Coarsely chopped peeled seeded tomato, about 15 lbs., 6.8 kg (see Tip, page 129)	18 cups	4.5 L
Olive (or cooking) oil	1 tsp.	5 mL
Chopped onion	1 cup	250 mL
Garlic cloves, minced (or 3/4 tsp., 4 mL, powder)	3	3
Granulated sugar	2 tsp.	10 mL
Salt	1 1/2 tsp.	7 mL
Pepper	1/8 tsp.	0.5 mL
Chopped fresh basil (or 1 tbsp., 15 mL, dried)	1/4 cup	60 mL
Chopped fresh oregano (or 3/4 tsp., 4 mL, dried)	1 tbsp.	15 mL

Process 9 cups (2.25 L) tomato in blender or food processor in batches until smooth.

Heat olive oil in Dutch oven on medium. Add onion and garlic. Cook for about 5 minutes, stirring often, until softened.

Add next 3 ingredients, remaining tomato and processed tomato. Stir. Bring to a boil, stirring occasionally. Reduce heat to medium. Boil gently, uncovered, for about 1 hour, stirring occasionally, until reduced and thickened.

Add basil and oregano. Stir. Fill clean plastic containers to within 1/2 inch (12 mm) of top (see Tip, page 79). Wipe rims. Let stand at room temperature until cool. Cover with tight-fitting lids. Store in freezer for up to 6 months. Makes about 12 1/2 cups (3.1 L).

1/4 cup (60 mL): 15 Calories; 0 g Total Fat (0 g Mono, 0 g Poly, 0 g Sat); 0 mg Cholesterol; 3 g Carbohydrate; trace Fibre; trace Protein; 75 mg Sodium

Pictured on page 108.

CC Signature Hot Sauce

This hot sauce is so good that we just had to put our name on it! Thick and tomatoey with lots of hot chili seeds, and a hint of sweetness to balance the flavours out. This is the ultimate all-purpose hot sauce.

Can of crushed tomatoes	14 oz.	398 mL
Can of tomato sauce	14 oz.	398 mL
Chopped fresh hot chili pepper (see Tip, page 116)	1 cup	250 mL
Apple cider vinegar	1/2 cup	125 mL
Chopped onion	1/2 cup	125 mL
Brown sugar, packed	1/3 cup	75 mL
Coarse (pickling) salt	1 tsp.	5 mL
Garlic cloves, minced (or 1/2 tsp., 2 mL, powder)	2	2

Process all 8 ingredients in blender or food processor until smooth. Transfer to large saucepan. Bring to a boil, stirring occasionally. Fill 4 hot sterile 1 cup (250 mL) jars to within 1/2 inch (12 mm) of top. Remove air bubbles and adjust headspace if necessary. Wipe rims. Place hot metal lids on jars and screw on metal bands fingertip tight. Do not over-tighten. Process in boiling water bath for 20 minutes (see page 9). Remove jars. Let stand at room temperature until cool. Makes about 4 cups (1 L).

1 tbsp. (15 mL): 10 Calories; 0 g Total Fat (0 g Mono, 0 g Poly, 0 g Sat); 0 mg Cholesterol; 2 g Carbohydrate; 0 g Fibre; 0 g Protein; 85 mg Sodium

Peach Lemongrass Syrup

A thin, fragrant peach syrup with notes of citrus sweetness. Drizzle over fruit salad, cake and crepes, or use it in a trifle.

Chopped peeled peach (see Tip, page 129)	4 1/2 cups	1.1 L
Water	1/2 cup	125 mL
Chopped lemon grass, bulb only	1/3 cup	75 mL
Granulated sugar	1 cup	250 mL
Bottled lemon juice	1 tsp.	5 mL

Combine first 3 ingredients in large saucepan. Bring to a boil, stirring occasionally. Reduce heat to medium-low. Simmer, uncovered, for about 15 minutes, crushing occasionally with potato masher, until peach is softened. Carefully strain through fine sieve or colander lined with double layer of damp cheesecloth into large bowl. Let stand for 2 hours. Do not squeeze solids. Discard solids. Measure 2 cups (500 mL) juice into medium saucepan.

Add sugar and lemon juice. Stir. Bring to a boil, stirring constantly until sugar is dissolved. Reduce heat to medium. Boil gently, uncovered, for about 10 minutes, stirring occasionally, until slightly thickened. Fill hot sterile jars to within 1/4 inch (6 mm) of top. Wipe rims. Let stand at room temperature until cool. Cover with tight-fitting lids. Makes about 2 1/4 cups (550 mL).

1 tbsp. (15 mL): 40 Calories; 0 g Total Fat (0 g Mono, 0 g Poly, 0 g Sat); 0 mg Cholesterol; 10 g Carbohydrate; 0 g Fibre; 0 g Protein; 0 mg Sodium

Pomegranate Barbecue Sauce

Tart, tangy and sweet. This traditional-looking sauce gets its zippy edge from pomegranate. This is one sauce that'll be a surefire hit at your next summer barbecue!

Pomegranate juice	4 cups	1 L
Chopped seeded tomato	16 cups	4 L
Chopped onion	2 cups	500 mL
Brown sugar, packed	1 1/2 cups	375 mL
White wine vinegar	1 cup	250 mL
Garlic cloves, minced	4	4
Dry mustard	1 tbsp.	15 mL
Coarse (pickling) salt	2 tsp.	10 mL
Dried crushed chilies	1/2 tsp.	2 mL
Ground cinnamon	1/2 tsp.	2 mL
Ground allspice	1/4 tsp.	1 mL

Measure pomegranate juice into Dutch oven. Bring to a boil, stirring occasionally. Reduce heat to medium. Boil gently, uncovered, for about 40 minutes, stirring occasionally, until reduced to about 1 cup (250 mL).

Process remaining 10 ingredients in blender or food processor in batches until smooth. Add to pomegranate juice. Stir. Bring to a boil, stirring occasionally. Reduce heat to medium. Boil gently, uncovered, for about 1 hour, stirring often, until reduced and thickened. Fill 5 hot sterile 2 cup (500 mL) jars to within 1/2 inch (12 mm) of top. Remove air bubbles and adjust headspace if necessary. Wipe rims. Place hot metal lids on jars and screw on metal bands fingertip tight. Do not over-tighten. Process in boiling water bath for 25 minutes (see page 9). Remove jars. Let stand at room temperature until cool. Makes about 10 1/4 cups (2.5 L).

2 tbsp. (30 mL): 30 Calories; 0 g Total Fat (0 g Mono, 0 g Poly, 0 g Sat); 0 mg Cholesterol; 7 g Carbohydrate; 0 g Fibre; 0 g Protein; 60 mg Sodium

Curried Fruit Sauce

This sweet and tangy curry sauce is nicely speckled with spices. It makes a perfect gift for the holidays because it pairs well with many popular holiday offerings, such as turkey or baked ham.

Orange juice	3 cups	750 mL
Chopped peeled apricot (see Tip, page 129)	1 2/3 cups	400 mL
Coarsely chopped peeled tart apple (such as Granny Smith)	1 1/2 cups	375 mL
Coarsely chopped onion	1 cup	250 mL
White corn syrup	3/4 cup	175 mL
Apple cider vinegar	1/2 cup	125 mL
Cumin seed	1 tbsp.	15 mL
Curry powder	1 tbsp.	15 mL
Salt	1 1/2 tsp.	7 mL
Dried crushed chilies	1/4 tsp.	1 mL
Ground allspice	1/4 tsp.	1 mL
Finely chopped fresh (or frozen) rhubarb	1 cup	250 mL
Chopped golden raisins	1/2 cup	125 mL
Minced crystallized ginger	2 tbsp.	30 mL

Process first 4 ingredients in food processor until smooth. Transfer to Dutch oven.

Add next 7 ingredients. Bring to a boil, stirring occasionally. Reduce heat to medium. Boil gently, uncovered, for 10 minutes, stirring occasionally.

Add rhubarb and raisins. Stir. Boil gently, uncovered, for about 15 minutes, stirring often, until thickened.

Stir in ginger. Fill 5 hot sterile 1 cup (250 mL) jars to within 1/4 inch (6 mm) of top. Remove air bubbles and adjust headspace if necessary. Wipe rims. Place hot metal lids on jars and screw on metal bands fingertip tight. Do not over-tighten. Process in boiling water bath for 15 minutes (see page 9). Remove jars. Let stand at room temperature until cool. Makes about 5 2/3 cups (1.4 L).

2 tbsp. (30 mL): 40 Calories; 0 g Total Fat (0 g Mono, 0 g Poly, 0 g Sat); 0 mg Cholesterol; 9 g Carbohydrate; trace Fibre; 0 g Protein; 85 mg Sodium

Southwest Barbecue Sauce

Smoky barbecue sauce with a chipotle kick. Great on barbecued chicken and spareribs, or as a spread on Mexican wraps.

Cooking oil	2 tsp.	10 mL
Chopped onion	1 1/2 cups	375 mL
Chopped green pepper	1/2 cup	125 mL
Garlic cloves, minced (or 1/2 tsp., 2 mL, powder)	2	2
Ketchup	1 1/2 cups	375 mL
Bottled lemon juice	1/2 cup	125 mL
Brown sugar, packed	1/2 cup	125 mL
Worcestershire sauce	1 tbsp.	15 mL
Chili powder	2 tsp.	10 mL
Ground cumin	2 tsp.	10 mL
Finely chopped chipotle peppers in adobo sauce (see Tip, page 94)	1 tsp.	5 mL

Heat cooking oil in large saucepan on medium. Add next 3 ingredients. Cook for about 8 minutes, stirring often, until onion and green pepper are softened.

Add remaining 7 ingredients. Stir. Bring to a boil. Reduce heat to medium-low. Simmer, uncovered, for 10 minutes, stirring often, to blend flavours. Carefully process in blender until smooth (see Safety Tip). Fill 3 hot sterile 1 cup (250 mL) jars to within 1/4 inch (6 mm) of top. Remove air bubbles and adjust headspace if necessary. Wipe rims. Place hot metal lids on jars and screw on metal bands fingertip tight. Do not over-tighten. Process in boiling water bath for 20 minutes (see page 9). Remove jars. Let stand at room temperature until cool. Makes about 3 cups (750 mL).

2 tbsp. (30 mL): 40 Calories; 0.5 g Total Fat (0 g Mono, 0 g Poly, 0 g Sat); 0 mg Cholesterol; 10 g Carbohydrate; 0 g Fibre; 0 g Protein; 200 mg Sodium

Safety Tip: Follow manufacturer's instructions for processing hot liquids.

Pear Brandy Syrup

Aromatic and mildly sweet. This is one recipe that really allows fresh pear flavour to shine, with brandy providing a nice background flavour on the finish.

Chopped peeled pear	8 cups	2 L
Water	1 cup	250 mL
Granulated sugar	1 cup	250 mL
Bottled lemon juice	2 tbsp.	30 mL
Brandy	1/4 cup	60 mL

Combine pear and water in Dutch oven. Bring to a boil. Reduce heat to medium. Boil gently, covered, for about 25 minutes, crushing occasionally with potato masher, until pear is softened. Carefully strain through fine sieve or colander lined with double layer of damp cheesecloth into large bowl. Let stand for 2 hours. Do not squeeze solids. Discard solids. Measure 3 cups (750 mL) juice into large saucepan.

Add sugar and lemon juice. Stir. Bring to a boil, stirring constantly until sugar is dissolved. Reduce heat to medium. Boil gently, uncovered, for about 35 minutes until thickened to syrup consistency.

Stir in brandy. Fill 5 hot sterile 1/2 cup (125 mL) jars to within 1/4 inch (6 mm) of top. Wipe rims. Place hot metal lids on jars and screw on metal bands fingertip tight. Do not over-tighten. Process in boiling water bath for 15 minutes (see page 9). Remove jars. Let stand at room temperature until cool. Makes about 2 2/3 cups (650 mL).

1 tbsp. (15 mL): 40 Calories; 0 g Total Fat (0 g Mono, 0 g Poly, 0 g Sat); 0 mg Cholesterol; 9 g Carbohydrate; trace Fibre; 0 g Protein; 0 mg Sodium

Bumbleberry Sauce

Capture the flavours of summer in this sweet-tart blend of berries in a luscious sauce. Perfect for serving over ice cream, angel food cake, yogurt or granola. Use any mix of berries as long as the total volume adds up to 4 1/2 cups (1.1 L).

Fresh blueberries (or saskatoon berries)	1 1/2 cups	375 mL
Fresh (or frozen) raspberries	1 1/2 cups	375 mL
Halved fresh strawberries	1 1/2 cups	375 mL
Mixed berry juice (no sugar added)	1 cup	250 mL
Grated lemon zest	1 tsp.	5 mL
Granulated sugar	3/4 cup	175 mL
Corn syrup	1/3 cup	75 mL
Bottled lemon juice	3 tbsp.	45 mL

Combine first 5 ingredients in large saucepan. Bring to a boil on medium, crushing occasionally with potato masher to break up berries.

Add sugar, stirring constantly until dissolved.

Add corn syrup and lemon juice. Bring to a hard boil, stirring constantly. Boil hard for 5 minutes, stirring often. Fill 4 hot sterile 1 cup (250 mL) jars to within 1/4 inch (6 mm) of top. Remove air bubbles and adjust headspace if necessary. Wipe rims. Place hot metal lids on jars and screw on metal bands fingertip tight. Do not over-tighten. Process in boiling water bath for 15 minutes (see page 9). Remove jars. Let stand at room temperature until cool. Makes about 4 1/2 cups (1.1 L).

2 tbsp. (30 mL): 35 Calories; 0 g Total Fat (0 g Mono, 0 g Poly, 0 g Sat); 0 mg Cholesterol; 9 g Carbohydrate; trace Fibre; 0 g Protein; 0 mg Sodium

Blueberry Vanilla Syrup

The perfect topping for pancakes, waffles or ice cream. If you have access to a saskatoon berry patch, try substituting saskatoons for some or all of the blueberries.

Fresh (or frozen) blueberries	10 cups	2.5 L
Water	1 cup	250 mL
Granulated sugar	2 cups	500 mL
Water	2 cups	500 mL
White corn syrup	1/3 cup	75 mL
Bottled lemon juice	2 tbsp.	30 mL
Vanilla extract	2 tsp.	10 mL

Combine blueberries and water in Dutch oven. Bring to a boil, stirring occasionally. Reduce heat to medium-low. Simmer, uncovered, for about 10 minutes, crushing occasionally with potato masher, until softened. Remove from heat. Carefully strain through fine sieve or colander lined with double layer of damp cheesecloth into large bowl. Let stand for 2 hours. Do not squeeze solids. Discard solids. Measure 2 cups (500 mL) juice into small bowl.

Combine sugar and water in large saucepan. Heat and stir on medium until sugar is dissolved. Bring to a boil, stirring constantly.

Add corn syrup and blueberry juice. Stir. Bring to a boil. Boil for 5 minutes. Remove from heat.

Stir in lemon juice and vanilla. Fill 5 hot sterile 1 cup (250 mL) jars to within 1/4 inch (6 mm) of top. Wipe rims. Place hot metal lids on jars and screw on metal bands fingertip tight. Do not over-tighten. Process in boiling water bath for 15 minutes (see page 9). Remove jars. Let stand at room temperature until cool. Makes about 5 cups (1.25 L).

1 tbsp. (15 mL): 30 Calories; 0 g Total Fat (0 g Mono, 0 g Poly, 0 g Sat); 0 mg Cholesterol; 8 g Carbohydrate; 0 g Fibre; 0 g Protein; 0 mg Sodium

Spicy Asparagus Spears

*These hot and smoky asparagus spears make a great addition to
a Caesar or Bloody Mary. For best results, select asparagus that are not
too thick or too thin.*

Fresh asparagus, trimmed of tough ends	3 lbs.	1.4 kg
Ice water, to cover		
White vinegar	2 1/2 cups	625 mL
Granulated sugar	1 cup	250 mL
Water	1 cup	250 mL
Coarse (pickling) salt	2 tsp.	10 mL
Finely chopped chipotle peppers	1 tsp.	5 mL
in adobo sauce (see Tip, page 94)		
Whole black peppercorns	2 tsp.	10 mL
Thinly sliced fresh hot red chili pepper	2 tsp.	10 mL
(see Tip, page 116)		

Cut asparagus to fit into 2 cup (500 mL) jars, leaving about 1 inch (2.5 cm)
headspace (see Note). Place asparagus in large bowl. Add ice water to cover.
Chill for 1 hour. Drain.

Combine next 5 ingredients in Dutch oven. Bring to a boil, stirring
occasionally. Boil, uncovered, for 5 minutes. Add asparagus. Stir. Cook for
about 1 minute until asparagus is heated through. Using slotted spoon,
transfer asparagus to medium bowl.

Divide peppercorns and chili pepper into 2 hot sterile 2 cup (500 mL) jars.
Pack asparagus, tip-side down, in jars to within 1 inch (2.5 cm) of top. Add
hot vinegar mixture to within 1/2 inch (12 mm) of top. Remove air bubbles
and adjust headspace if necessary. Discard any remaining vinegar mixture.
Wipe rims. Place hot metal lids on jars and screw on metal bands fingertip
tight. Do not over-tighten. Process in boiling water bath for 15 minutes (see
page 9). Turn off heat. Let stand, uncovered, for 5 minutes. Remove jars.
Let stand at room temperature until cool. Makes about 3 1/2 cups (875 mL).

*1 spear: 10 Calories; 0 g Total Fat (0 g Mono, 0 g Poly, 0 g Sat); 0 mg Cholesterol; 3 g Carbohydrate;
0 g Fibre; 0 g Protein; 45 mg Sodium*

Note: Reserve your asparagus trimmings for another use. They make a great
addition to soups.

Fig Cherry Leek Spread

Though the combination may seem a little unlikely, we assure you that this sweet-and-savoury combination is delicious. A very versatile spread that can be served on crackers or brie cheese, or with roast meat or grilled chicken.

Chopped fresh figs	3 cups	750 mL
Brown sugar, packed	2 cups	500 mL
Chopped dried cherries	1/4 cup	60 mL
Bottled lemon juice	3 tbsp.	45 mL
White wine vinegar	2 tbsp.	30 mL
Salt	1/8 tsp.	0.5 mL
Cooking oil	1 tsp.	5 mL
Thinly sliced leek (white part only)	1 cup	250 mL

Combine first 6 ingredients in large bowl. Let stand, covered, for 1 hour, stirring occasionally.

Heat cooking oil in large saucepan on medium. Add leek. Cook for about 5 minutes, stirring often, until softened. Add fig mixture. Stir. Cook, uncovered, for about 10 minutes, stirring occasionally, until mixture comes to a hard boil. Boil hard for about 10 minutes, stirring often, until mixture gels when tested on small cold plate (see Tip, page 77). Fill 3 hot sterile 1 cup (250 mL) jars to within 1/4 inch (6 mm) of top. Remove air bubbles and adjust headspace if necessary. Wipe rims. Place hot metal lids on jars and screw on metal bands fingertip tight. Do not over-tighten. Process in boiling water bath for 15 minutes (see page 9). Remove jars. Let stand at room temperature until cool. Makes about 3 cups (750 mL).

1 tbsp. (15 mL): 45 Calories; 0 g Total Fat (0 g Mono, 0 g Poly, 0 g Sat); 0 mg Cholesterol; 12 g Carbohydrate; 0 g Fibre; 0 g Protein; 10 mg Sodium

Grapefruit Wine Jelly

With only four ingredients, there's simply no excuse for not making your own homemade preserves! Serve with cheese, crackers or scones.

Unsweetened red (or pink) grapefruit juice	1 cup	250 mL
Dry white wine	1 cup	250 mL
Granulated sugar	3 1/2 cups	875 mL
Pouch of liquid pectin	3 oz.	85 mL

Combine first 3 ingredients in large saucepan. Bring to a hard boil, stirring constantly.

Add pectin. Boil hard for 2 minutes, stirring constantly. Fill 7 hot sterile 1/2 cup (125 mL) jars to within 1/4 inch (6 mm) of top. Remove air bubbles and adjust headspace if necessary. Wipe rims. Place hot metal lids on jars and screw on metal bands fingertip tight. Do not over-tighten. Process in boiling water bath for 15 minutes (see page 9). Remove jars. Let stand at room temperature until cool. Makes about 3 2/3 cups (900 mL).

1 tbsp. (15 mL): 50 Calories; 0 g Total Fat (0 g Mono, 0 g Poly, 0 g Sat); 0 mg Cholesterol; 12 g Carbohydrate; 0 g Fibre; 0 g Protein; 0 mg Sodium

Pictured on page 143.

1. Grapefruit Wine Jelly, above
2. Spicy Tequila Lime Jelly, page 78

Small Batch

Almond Honey Cherries

Sweet cherries and almond liqueur create a complex flavour combination. This elegant and sophisticated preserve makes a classy topping for the very best vanilla ice cream.

Water	1 cup	250 mL
Liquid honey	1/2 cup	125 mL
Pitted sweet cherries	3 1/2 cups	875 mL
Almond liqueur	3 tbsp.	50 mL

Combine water and honey in large saucepan. Bring to a boil, stirring often.

Add cherries. Reduce heat to medium. Cook, uncovered, for 5 minutes, stirring occasionally. Using slotted spoon, fill 3 hot sterile 1 cup (250 mL) jars with cherries to within 1 inch (2.5 cm) of top.

Add liqueur to hot honey mixture. Stir. Add to jars to within 1/2 inch (12 mm) of top. Remove air bubbles and adjust headspace if necessary. Discard any remaining honey mixture. Wipe rims. Place hot metal lids on jars and screw on metal bands fingertip tight. Do not over-tighten. Process in boiling water bath for 15 minutes (see page 9). Turn off heat. Let stand, uncovered, for 5 minutes. Remove jars. Let stand at room temperature until cool. Makes about 3 cups (750 mL).

2 tbsp. (30 mL): 35 Calories; 0 g Total Fat 0 g Mono, 0 g Poly, 0 g Sat); 0 mg Cholesterol; 9 g Carbohydrate; 0 g Fibre; 0 g Protein; 0 mg Sodium

Pictured on page 144.

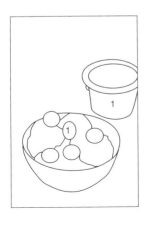

1. Almond Honey Cherries, above

Blueberry Orange Freezer Jam

This freezer jam is equally delicious with fresh or frozen blueberries. If you've got berries on hand in the summer, try the fresh version. With frozen berries, you'll get a deep blueberry flavour. It's a win-win situation!

Granulated sugar	3/4 cup	175 mL
Envelope of freezer jam pectin, 1.59 oz., 45 g (see Note)	1/2	1/2
Crushed fresh blueberries	1 1/2 cups	375 mL
Finely chopped orange segments (see Tip, below)	1/2 cup	125 mL
Orange liqueur	1 tbsp.	15 mL
Grated orange zest (see Tip, page 31)	1 tsp.	5 mL

Combine sugar and pectin in medium bowl.

Add remaining 4 ingredients. Stir for 3 minutes. Fill clean plastic containers to within 1/2 inch (12 mm) of top (see Tip, page 79). Wipe rims. Let stand at room temperature for about 30 minutes until thickened. Cover with tight-fitting lids. Store in refrigerator for up to 3 weeks or in freezer for up to 1 year. Makes about 2 1/4 cups (550 mL).

1 tbsp. (15 mL): 20 Calories; 0 g Total Fat (0 g Mono, 0 g Poly, 0 g Sat); 0 mg Cholesterol; 5 g Carbohydrate; 0 g Fibre; 0 g Protein; 0 mg Sodium

Note: Double the recipe to use the entire envelope of pectin, or use the remaining pectin to make Mango Kiwi Freezer Jam, page 151.

 tip

To segment citrus fruits, trim a small slice of peel from both ends so the flesh is exposed. Place the fruit, bottom cut-side down, on a cutting board. Remove the peel with a sharp knife, cutting down and around the flesh, leaving as little pith as possible. Over a small bowl, cut on either side of the membranes to release the segments.

Kohlrabi Fennel Giardiniera

A colourful blend of pickled vegetables. A little sweetness, a bit of spicy heat and a touch of herb flavour make these pickles a flavourful condiment for sandwiches, or a great accompaniment for barbecue fare.

Thinly sliced fennel bulb (white part only)	1 cup	250 mL
Thinly sliced kohlrabi, quartered	1 cup	250 mL
Chopped red pepper	3/4 cup	175 mL
Thinly sliced carrot	3/4 cup	175 mL
Chopped red onion	1/2 cup	125 mL
White vinegar	1 1/2 cups	375 mL
Granulated sugar	3/4 cup	175 mL
Water	1/2 cup	125 mL
Coarse (pickling) salt	1 tbsp.	15 mL
Garlic cloves, thinly sliced	2	2
Whole black peppercorns	1 tsp.	5 mL
Bay leaf	1	1
Dried oregano	1/2 tsp.	2 mL
Dried crushed chilies	1/4 tsp.	1 mL

Toss first 5 ingredients in medium bowl. Pack into sterile 4 cup (1 L) jar.

Combine remaining 9 ingredients in medium saucepan. Bring to a boil, stirring often. Reduce heat to medium-low. Simmer, covered, for 10 minutes. Pour over fennel mixture to cover. Let stand at room temperature until cool. Cover with tight-fitting lid. Chill for 1 day before opening. Store in refrigerator for up to 3 weeks. Makes about 4 cups (1 L).

1/4 cup (60 mL): 50 Calories; 0 g Total Fat (0 g Mono, 0 g Poly, 0 g Sat); 0 mg Cholesterol; 13 g Carbohydrate; trace Fibre; 0 g Protein; 440 mg Sodium

Quick Freezer Pickles

No one will ever guess that these zippy pickles came from your freezer.
They're simply too crisp and colourful and absolutely loaded with flavour
from ginger and onion!

Thinly sliced trimmed pickling cucumbers	5 cups	1.25 L
Thinly sliced onion	1 cup	250 mL
Coarse (pickling) salt	1 tbsp.	15 mL
White vinegar	2 cups	500 mL
Granulated sugar	1 cup	250 mL
Finely chopped ginger root	2 tsp.	10 mL
Mustard seed	2 tsp.	10 mL
Celery seed	1/2 tsp.	2 mL

Combine first 3 ingredients in large bowl. Let stand, covered, at room temperature for 3 hours. Drain. Rinse with cold water. Drain well. Fill clean plastic containers with cucumber mixture to within 1 inch (2.5 cm) of top (see Tip, page 79).

Combine remaining 5 ingredients in small saucepan. Bring to a boil, stirring constantly. Reduce heat to medium-low. Simmer, covered, for 10 minutes. Pour over cucumber mixture to within 1/2 inch (12 mm) of top. Discard any remaining vinegar mixture. Wipe rims. Let stand until cool. Cover with tight-fitting lids. Store in freezer for up to 6 months. Store in refrigerator for up to 5 days after opening. Makes about 5 cups (1.25 L).

1/4 cup (60 mL): 50 Calories; 0 g Total Fat (0 g Mono, 0 g Poly, 0 g Sat); 0 mg Cholesterol;
13 g Carbohydrate; 0 g Fibre; 0 g Protein; 340 mg Sodium

Freezer Bruschetta

*A quick and easy way to preserve your garden tomatoes—and you'll have
a flavourful, versatile bruschetta ready and waiting in your freezer!*

Olive (or cooking) oil	1 tsp.	5 mL
Finely chopped red onion	1/2 cup	125 mL
Garlic cloves, minced	3	3
Chopped seeded Roma (plum) tomato	3 cups	750 mL
Chopped fresh basil leaves, lightly packed	1 cup	250 mL
Chopped fresh oregano (or 1/4 tsp., 1 mL, dried)	2 tbsp.	30 mL
Olive (or cooking) oil	2 tbsp.	30 mL
Red wine vinegar	2 tbsp.	30 mL
Brown sugar, packed	2 tsp.	10 mL
Salt	1/4 tsp.	1 mL
Pepper	1/4 tsp.	1 mL

Heat first amount of olive oil in large saucepan on medium. Add onion
and garlic. Cook for about 5 minutes, stirring occasionally, until onion is
softened.

Add remaining 8 ingredients. Stir. Bring to a boil, stirring occasionally.
Fill clean plastic containers to within 1/2 inch (12 mm) of top (see Tip,
page 79). Wipe rims. Let stand at room temperature until cool. Cover
with tight-fitting lids. Store in refrigerator for up to 1 week or in freezer
for up to 1 month. Makes about 2 3/4 cups (675 mL).

*1 tbsp. (15 mL): 10 Calories; 0.5 g Total Fat (0.5 g Mono, 0 g Poly, 0 g Sat); 0 mg Cholesterol;
1 g Carbohydrate; 0 g Fibre; 0 g Protein; 15 mg Sodium*

Tomato Balsamic Jam

This dark, jewel-toned jam with rich tomato flavour is good for spreading onto crackers with cheese (especially goat cheese!), or as a sandwich condiment.

Can of plum tomatoes, drained and seeds removed	28 oz.	796 mL
Granulated sugar	3/4 cup	175 mL
Sun-dried tomatoes, softened in boiling water for 10 minutes, chopped	3/4 cup	175 mL
Balsamic vinegar	1/2 cup	125 mL
Dried thyme	1 tsp.	5 mL
Salt	1 tsp.	5 mL
Pepper	1 tsp.	5 mL

Combine all 7 ingredients in medium saucepan. Bring to a boil, stirring occasionally. Reduce heat to medium-low. Simmer, uncovered, for about 50 minutes, stirring occasionally, until thickened. Carefully process in blender or food processor until coarsely chopped (see Safety Tip). Fill 4 hot sterile 1/2 cup (125 mL) jars to within 1/2 inch (12 mm) of top. Remove air bubbles and adjust headspace if necessary. Wipe rims. Place hot metal lids on jars and screw on metal bands fingertip tight. Do not over-tighten. Process in boiling water bath for 15 minutes (see page 9). Remove jars. Let stand at room temperature until cool. Makes about 2 cups (500 mL).

1 tbsp. (15 mL): 30 Calories; 0 g Total Fat (0 g Mono, 0 g Poly, 0 g Sat); 0 mg Cholesterol; 7 g Carbohydrate; 0 g Fibre; 0 g Protein; 150 mg Sodium

Safety Tip: Follow manufacturer's instructions for processing hot liquids.

Small Batch

Mango Kiwi Freezer Jam

This freezer jam is a delightful option for those who aren't willing to commit to a big batch, nor to all the hassle of processing. Make this jam with fresh mango for optimal flavour and texture.

Granulated sugar	3/4 cup	175 mL
Envelope of freezer jam pectin, 1.59 oz., 45 g (see Note)	1/2	1/2
Finely chopped ripe mango	1 cup	250 mL
Finely chopped kiwi fruit	1/2 cup	125 mL
Chopped grapefruit segments (see Tip, page 146)	1/2 cup	125 mL
Grated grapefruit zest (see Tip, page 31)	1/2 tsp.	2 mL

Combine sugar and pectin in medium bowl.

Add remaining 4 ingredients. Stir for 3 minutes. Fill clean plastic containers to within 1/2 inch (12 mm) of top (see Tip, page 79). Wipe rims. Let stand at room temperature for about 30 minutes until thickened. Cover with tight-fitting lids. Store in refrigerator for up to 3 weeks or in freezer for up to 1 year. Makes about 2 cups (500 mL).

1 tbsp. (15 mL): 25 Calories; 0 g Total Fat (0 g Mono, 0 g Poly, 0 g Sat); 0 mg Cholesterol; 6 g Carbohydrate; 0 g Fibre; 0 g Protein; 0 mg Sodium

Pictured on page 107.

Note: Double the recipe to use the entire envelope of pectin, or use the remaining pectin to make Blueberry Orange Freezer Jam, page 146.

Measurement Tables

Throughout this book measurements are given in Conventional and Metric measure. To compensate for differences between the two measurements due to rounding, a full metric measure is not always used. The cup used is the standard 8 fluid ounce. Temperature is given in degrees Fahrenheit and Celsius. Baking pan measurements are in inches and centimetres as well as quarts and litres. An exact metric conversion is given below as well as the working equivalent (Metric Standard Measure).

Spoons

Conventional Measure	Metric Exact Conversion Millilitre (mL)	Metric Standard Measure Millilitre (mL)
1/8 teaspoon (tsp.)	0.6 mL	0.5 mL
1/4 teaspoon (tsp.)	1.2 mL	1 mL
1/2 teaspoon (tsp.)	2.4 mL	2 mL
1 teaspoon (tsp.)	4.7 mL	5 mL
2 teaspoons (tsp.)	9.4 mL	10 mL
1 tablespoon (tbsp.)	14.2 mL	15 mL

Cups

Conventional Measure	Metric Exact Conversion Millilitre (mL)	Metric Standard Measure Millilitre (mL)
1/4 cup (4 tbsp.)	56.8 mL	60 mL
1/3 cup (5 1/3 tbsp.)	75.6 mL	75 mL
1/2 cup (8 tbsp.)	113.7 mL	125 mL
2/3 cup (10 2/3 tbsp.)	151.2 mL	150 mL
3/4 cup (12 tbsp.)	170.5 mL	175 mL
1 cup (16 tbsp.)	227.3 mL	250 mL
4 1/2 cups	1022.9 mL	1000 mL (1 L)

Dry Measurements

Conventional Measure Ounces (oz.)	Metric Exact Conversion Grams (g)	Metric Standard Measure Grams (g)
1 oz.	28.3 g	28 g
2 oz.	56.7 g	57 g
3 oz.	85.0 g	85 g
4 oz.	113.4 g	125 g
5 oz.	141.7 g	140 g
6 oz.	170.1 g	170 g
7 oz.	198.4 g	200 g
8 oz.	226.8 g	250 g
16 oz.	453.6 g	500 g
32 oz.	907.2 g	1000 g (1 kg)

Oven Temperatures

Fahrenheit (°F)	Celsius (°C)
175°	80°
200°	95°
225°	110°
250°	120°
275°	140°
300°	150°
325°	160°
350°	175°
375°	190°
400°	205°
425°	220°
450°	230°
475°	240°
500°	260°

Pans

Conventional Inches	Metric Centimetres
8x8 inch	20x20 cm
9x9 inch	23x23 cm
9x13 inch	23x33 cm
10x15 inch	25x38 cm
11x17 inch	28x43 cm
8x2 inch round	20x5 cm
9x2 inch round	23x5 cm
10x4 1/2 inch tube	25x11 cm
8x4x3 inch loaf	20x10x7.5 cm
9x5x3 inch loaf	23x12.5x7.5 cm

Casseroles

CANADA & BRITAIN Standard Size Casserole	Exact Metric Measure	UNITED STATES Standard Size Casserole	Exact Metric Measure
1 qt. (5 cups)	1.13 L	1 qt. (4 cups)	900 mL
1 1/2 qts. (7 1/2 cups)	1.69 L	1 1/2 qts. (6 cups)	1.35 L
2 qts. (10 cups)	2.25 L	2 qts. (8 cups)	1.8 L
2 1/2 qts. (12 1/2 cups)	2.81 L	2 1/2 qts. (10 cups)	2.25 L
3 qts. (15 cups)	3.38 L	3 qts. (12 cups)	2.7 L
4 qts. (20 cups)	4.5 L	4 qts. (16 cups)	3.6 L
5 qts. (25 cups)	5.63 L	5 qts. (20 cups)	4.5 L

Recipe Index

153

155

P

Q

R

157

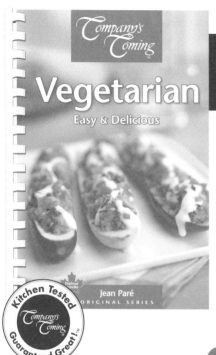

Vegetarian

Vegetarian food is more than meaty food's bland cousin, and you don't have to be a vegetarian to enjoy it. Full of tasty vegetables, grains, legumes, nuts and seeds, it usually has less saturated fat and more fibre and antioxidants than meaty meals. The whole family will love these healthy recipes, and even die-hard meat eaters won't miss the meat.

Try it

a sample recipe from *Vegetarian*, page 16

Root Vegetable Tapenade

Fresh medium beet, (about 8 oz., 225 g) scrubbed clean and trimmed	1	1
Small fennel bulb (about 7 oz., 200 g), halved	1	1
Small onion (about 6 oz., 170 g), halved	1	1
Crumbled blue cheese (optional)	2 tbsp.	30 mL
Chopped fresh chives	1 tbsp.	15 mL
Olive (or cooking) oil	1 tbsp.	15 mL
Balsamic vinegar	1 tbsp.	15 mL
Salt	1/8 tsp.	0.5 mL
Pepper, sprinkle		
Chopped fresh chives	1 tsp.	5 mL

Wrap beet, fennel and onion individually with foil. Bake on foil-lined baking sheet with sides in 375°F (190°C) oven for about 1 hour until tender.

Discard foil. Let stand for about 5 minutes until cool enough to handle. Peel and chop beet. Chop fennel and onion. Transfer to food processor.

Add next 6 ingredients. Process using on/off motion until vegetables are coarsely chopped.

Sprinkle with second amount of chives. Makes about 2 cups (500 mL).

1/4 cup (60 mL): 50 Calories; 2.5 g Total Fat (1.5 g Mono, 0 g Poly, 0.5 g Sat); 0 mg Cholesterol; 7 g Carbohydrate; 2 g Fibre; 1 g Protein; 100 mg Sodium

Celebrating the
Harvest
RECIPES FOR FALL & WINTER GATHERINGS

Whether from the garden, farmers' market or supermarket, harvest ingredients display the bounty and beauty of nature. Entertain a crowd in style, or feed your family comfort food they'll not soon forget—with new delicious recipes that celebrate harvest ingredients. What a lovely way to get through the long fall and winter!

SPECIAL OCCASION SERIES

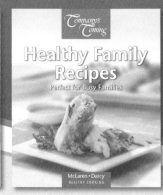